SOFTWARE ERGONOMICS
Advances and Applications

ELLIS HORWOOD BOOKS IN COMPUTING SCIENCE

General Editors: Professor JOHN CAMPBELL, University College London, and BRIAN L. MEEK, Director of Information Technology, Goldsmiths' College, London, and King's College London (KQC), University of London

Series in Computers and Their Applications

Series Editor: BRIAN L. MEEK, Director of Information Technology, Goldsmiths' College, London, and King's College London (KQC), University of London

Series continued at end of book

SOFTWARE ERGONOMICS
Advances and Applications

Editors:
H.-J. BULLINGER
Professor of Human Factors, University of Stuttgart, and
Head of the Fraunhofer Institute for Industrial Engineering, Stuttgart, FRG

and

R. GUNZENHÄUSER
Professor of Computer Science
University of Stuttgart, FRG

Translator:
D. LEWIS
School of Modern Languages, University of Exeter

ELLIS HORWOOD LIMITED
Publishers · Chichester

Halsted Press: a division of
JOHN WILEY & SONS
New York · Chichester · Brisbane · Toronto

This English edition first published in 1988 by
ELLIS HORWOOD LIMITED
Market Cross House, Cooper Street,
Chichester, West Sussex, PO19 1EB, England
The publisher's colophon is reproduced from James Gillison's drawing of the ancient Market Cross, Chichester.

Distributors:

Australia and New Zealand:
JACARANDA WILEY LIMITED
GPO Box 859, Brisbane, Queensland 4001, Australia

Canada:
JOHN WILEY & SONS CANADA LIMITED
22 Worcester Road, Rexdale, Ontario, Canada

Europe and Africa:
JOHN WILEY & SONS LIMITED
Baffins Lane, Chichester, West Sussex, England

North and South America and the rest of the world:
Halsted Press: a division of
JOHN WILEY & SONS
605 Third Avenue, New York, NY 10158, USA

This English edition is translated from the original German edition *Software-Ergonomie*, published in 1986 by Expert Verlag, © the copyright holders.

© **1988 English Edition, Ellis Horwood Limited**

British Library Cataloguing in Publication Data
Software ergonomics: advances and applications. —
(Ellis Horwood books in computer science).
1. Computer systems. Software. Design.
I. Bullinger, Hans-Jorg   II. Gunzenhauser, R. (Rul)
III. Software-Ergonomie. *English*
005'.1.2

Library of Congress CIP data available

ISBN 0–7458–0283–4 (Ellis Horwood Limited)
ISBN 0–470–21177–6 (Halsted Press)

Phototypeset in Times by Ellis Horwood Limited
Printed in Great Britain by Unwin Bros., Woking

Table of contents

Editor's Preface to the German Edition

Over the last few years we have seen the value of ongoing vocational education as a vital investment for the future. Because of the speed at which technology is changing and knowledge is being acquired, we are constantly having to absorb, process and implement the latest advances in research and development. A single training course or period of study is no longer enough to keep pace with events. Life-long learning in the form of ongoing vocational education is essential to meet our current and future needs.

The aims of vocational education are as follows:

(a) to enable us to keep pace with the latest research developments
(b) to widen our knowledge of other relevant fields
(c) to learn how to make practical use of scientific research
(d) to help human beings react positively towards their work and new technology.

Attending training courses and keeping up-to-date with specialist publications are the best ways of achieving these aims.

The present book originally appeared in German in a series entitled CONTACT & STUDY, a joint venture between the West German publishing company, Expert Verlag, and the Technical Academy of Esslingen (TAE).

The series was based on successful, practical and up-to-date courses for students at the TAE. Several authors — including scientists and practitioners in the field — have been involved in the production of this book, and we hope to have done justice to both theory and practice.

We hope that the book will do more than complement existing training courses. It should also be a valuable aid for those studying on their own and as a work of reference. The authors hope that it will not disappoint the reader who is looking for both depth and usefulness.

Professor Wilfried J. Bartz
Technical Academy of Esslingen

Elmar Wippler
Expert Verlag

Authors' Preface to the German Edition

For some years software ergonomics, as a topical and relatively new field, has attracted considerable discussion. Scientists and researchers in work study, information processing and psychology see software ergonomics as providing new challenges for interdisciplinary cooperation. Two specialist conferences — in Nuremburg (1983) and Stuttgart (1985) — presented the state of current research and pointed the way to future developments and applications.

In data processing, the science of software ergonomics was first applied to the development of equipment. The results could be seen in the better design of screen monitors, keyboards and other hardware for user interfaces. Software ergonomics therefore made a very positive contribution to the working conditions of those professionally involved in data processing.

Software ergonomics has now expanded to include the design of user-friendly software. Examples are screen-based dialogue techniques, so called user models, help systems and knowledge-based interaction. Related issues are users' acceptance of computer systems and the effects of computerisation in the office.

A general research goal of software ergonomics can legitimately be seen as developing ideas and methods which will give the user easier access to all the facilities which the computer has to offer.

Research into software ergonomics has already produced a number of important studies and a significant body of results. Despite this, there is still a shortfall between basic research and practical applications. This is why we try in this book to present some of the more scientific advances from the point of view of the user and to offer practical guidelines for designing dialogue-based user interfaces. A major emphasis is placed on models of knowledge-based communication between human beings and the computer.

All the contributions to this book are based on material for a course on software ergonomics at the Centre for Further Education at the Technical Academy of Esslingen. The course was first provided in 1984 for a number of professional people involved with computers. These included senior computer staff working with interactive dialogue systems, developers of application software with user interfaces, organisation and methods personnel, and training and managerial staff. The course was repeated in 1985.

Several authors have contributed to this book:

Hans-Jörg Bullinger, in his contribution on the fundamentals of dialogue design, describes in detail the major types of user interface; from these he develops a scientific model for ergonomic design. K. P. Fähnrich discusses forms of dialogue which are suitable for man–machine communication. Examples are command languages, screen displays with fixed data fields, menu systems, icons and pointers and natural language. J. Ziegler discusses concrete examples of screen-based dialogues, the design of signs, the use of symbols and the layout of information. H. von Benda reports on practical experiences encountered in implementing large application systems. She discusses intelligent workstations and gives examples of working systems in the field of public administration.

G. Fischer and M. Herczeg cover the basic principles of knowldge-based systems, illustrating them with practical examples from form processing and computer-assisted planning. R. Gunzenhäuser and Th. Knopik continue this theme, reporting on user models and help facilities which they illustrate by an intelligent tutor for a game strategy. H. Balzert's contribution provides a broad and systematic overview of current and future input and output devices for man–machine interaction, including human speech: we also see how these devices interact at a prototype office workplace.

Finally, W. Schweikhardt deals with experiences of designing user interfaces and tutorial programs which could help blind people in learning new skills and in their work.

The editors wish to thank the Technical Academy of Esslinglen and the publishers, Expert Verlag, for their interest in such a new and specialised field. We are grateful for the design of the book and the speed with which the German edition came into print. Furthermore, we express our sincere gratitude to the authors who have collaborated in research and development and for their teaching work at the University of Stuttgart. This book, which is entirely the product of team work, has done much to promote the already excellent cooperation between the Stuttgart Institute of Work Study and the Institute of Informatics.

H. J. Bullinger

Stuttgart, March 1986   R. Gunzenhäuser

1

Principles and illustrations of dialogue design

H.-J. Bullinger

1.1 FROM HARDWARE ERGONOMICS TO SOFTWARE ERGONOMICS

We can define ergonomics as follows:

> Ergonomics uses scientific methods to describe (a) human attributes and (b) work. Work is described in terms of its processes and environment, where it is done and how it is organised. The object is to adjust the nature of work to suit human characteristics. Our principal aim is, as far as possible, to avoid subjecting human beings to stress in their work and to ensure that they derive the maximum benefit from their abilities, skills, tools and resources.

The science of work study — especially ergonomics — was originally concerned with resources, the place of work, the environment and the organization of workflow. Fig. 1.1 shows the areas which have concerned

---

THE ERGONOMICS OF DESIGNING A COMPUTER SCREEN TERMINAL AND ITS FUNCTIONS

Concerned with the design and coordination of
— resources and equipment
— the place of work
— the environment
— the organisation of work

Resources–equipment	The workplace	The environment	Organisation
—the screen (VDU)	—desk	—lighting	—Content of work
—keyboard	—chair	—ventilation	—workflow
—documents	—footrest	—noise	—structure
—peripheral devices	—document holder	—general layout	—time
—other resources	—arrangement of resources		—software ergonomics

---

Fig. 1.1 — The ergonomics of designing a computer screen terminal and its functions.

ergonomists and the factors involved.

The results of research into ergonomics — especially into equipment and workplace design — are now well established and have led to changes in industrial standards and the law.

Users of computers, however, are finding themselves faced with increasingly more complex screen monitors. It is precisely for this type of equipment that we need to involve ergonomics at the early design stage (instead of trying to correct problems when the equipment is already in use).

Software ergonomics is primarily concerned with interfaces between the computer and its human user. These are encountered on the factory floor, in the office and at management level. Examples include numeric control machines, production control, computer-controlled manufacturing, data collection and processing systems, workflow planning, computer-aided design, document production, text processing, communications and information systems. What all these applications have in common is the need for a dialogue between the human user and the computer system. Software ergonomics has three main concerns: analysis, design and assessment (see Fig. 1.2).

Analysis of	Design of	Assessment of
— human attributes and capabilities in handling information	— the user interface for a computer system	— load–demands of the work situation
— tasks to be performed	— the presentation of information	— performance; also reactions to errors, quality of work and time taken
— current and future technology	— the dialogue between the user and the machine	— end user's acceptance of system

Fig. 1.2 — The function of software ergonomics.

1.2   MAN–MACHINE INTERFACE

The terms 'man–machine interface', 'human–computer interface' or 'user interface' are often used in connection with interactive systems, although up to now we have not defined exactly what we mean by them. On the one hand they refer to features which, in one form or another, are present in any interactive system. On the other hand they are applied to those modules of a system which enable information to be passed between the user and the actual application module (such as a data base).

Not every interactive system has a specific user interface which is clearly distinct from the application module. However, in terms of both software engineering and ergonomics, it makes sense to implement interfaces between the machine and its user independently of a particular application (as far as this is possible). By using standard interfaces for different applications (e.g. in an integrated office system), it is possible to keep development cost down and to maintain a consistent interface for the end user.

So-called user interface management systems (UIMS) are an aid to the design of user interfaces: they provide standardised tools such as windows, menus, editors for pictures and screen displays, and formal representations of dialogue syntax. While much current research activity is focused on the formal representation of dialogue, other UIMS components are already commercially available as software tools, despite a regrettable lack of standardisation. The experimental systems COUSIN [1,2] and XS-2 [3] illustrate the state of research, and there is also an interesting study by Coutaz [4].

The structural model which we present below is an attempt to integrate these approaches and to interpret man–machine communication in terms of a layered model similar to that of the International Standards Organisation Open Systems Interconnection (ISO OSI (see Fig. 1.3).

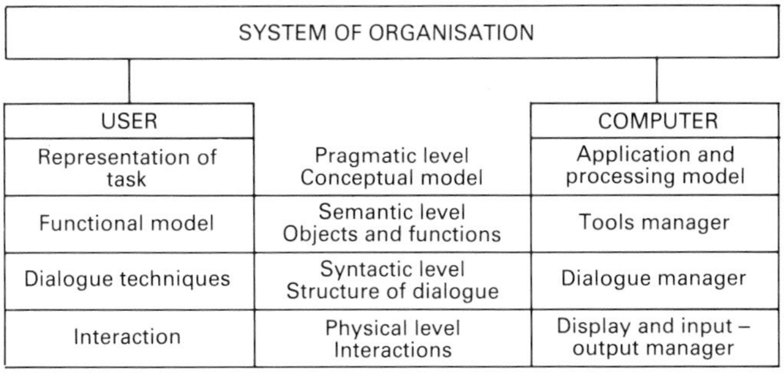

SYSTEM OF ORGANISATION		
USER		**COMPUTER**
Representation of task	Pragmatic level Conceptual model	Application and processing model
Functional model	Semantic level Objects and functions	Tools manager
Dialogue techniques	Syntactic level Structure of dialogue	Dialogue manager
Interaction	Physical level Interactions	Display and input – output manager

Fig 1.3 — A layered model for human–computer interfaces.

The model defines a framework for the tasks which are to be carried out by the human being and the computer. Communication is described in terms of four layers (or protocols according to the ISO OSI model) which are derived from modern communication theory.

Successful communication between a human being and the computer presupposes that compatible structures exist for each level or layer of the task and the dialogue. As one might expect, the structure of the task determines the structure and adequacy of the representation of the dialogue. There are formal, descriptive methods for representing dialogues. The reader is referred to Moran's command language grammar [5] and the GOMS model of Card et al. [6].

The input–output interface constitutes the sole physical link between the human being and the computer. It accepts user input from a keyboard, pointer or speech input device, etc. and converts it into a device-independent, functional representation (the dialogue interface) which is passed on to the dialogue system (*cf.* Fig. 1.4). In addition, the input–output system

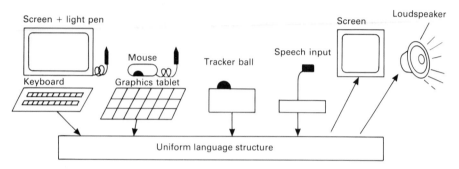

Fig. 1.4 — Implementing a device-independent input–output interface for various input systems.

also converts output from the dialogue interface into a coded form for a specific device (screen monitor, speech output device, etc.). Fig. 1.5

| Richard Meyer   : | SAMPLE SALES RECORD | : Date   : 01.02.84 |
| | FOR ORDER PROCESSING DEPARTMENT | : User   : JK |

Registration No:. . . . .   Order No: . . . .
                                                             Customer No: . . . .

Customer Address: Delivery address:

Name   :   . . . .
Street   :   . . . .
Town   :   . . . .
PO Code   :   . . . .
Country   :   . . . .

Attention: This is a specimen

. . . . Despatch data . . . .

Delivered from: . . . .   Your reference: . . . .
Terms of payment: . . . .   Account: . . . .
Currency: . . . .   Price: . . . .

<RETURN> = Continue   <F1> = Finish   <F2> = Stop

Fig. 1.5 — Example of screen mask for inputting data.

illustrates a typical screen display with fixed fields for inputting data.

The dialogue system performs a syntactic analysis of the inputs from the dialogue interface to formulate syntactically correct output sentences. The interface thus provides the entry parameters for the various software tools which, for the user, constitute the available functions of the computer. The dialogue representation at the interface level is independent of the dialogue system for the particular application which actually processes the data. This model proceeds from the conceptual level, through the semantic and syntactic level, to the interaction itself. System standardisation, incidentally, has taken the opposite direction.

1.3   HOW TO DESIGN DIALOGUE SYSTEMS

Fig. 1.6 shows a tried-and-tested procedure for designing human–computer

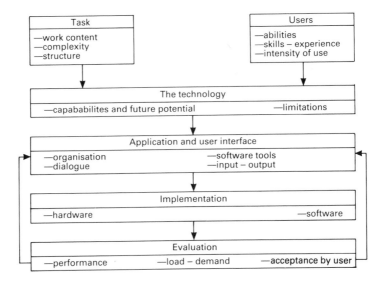

Fig. 1.6 — Procedure for the design of a user interface.

interfaces. After the analysis phase (which identifies the tasks, the users and the technology available), specifications are drawn up for the application and the user interface, which are then implemented. The system is finally evaluated. This procedure is repeated for as long as necessary.

The procedure can be refined in the light of the model for a human–computer interface described in section 1.2. This involves defining and drawing up specifications for the following (see Figs. 1.7–1.10 for details):

— the application and its representation
— the software tools and their representations
— the dialogue system
— the interaction, i.e. input–output system

Task analyses provide information about the content, complexity and structure of the work which is to be done.

Analysis of the users provides information about the capabilities and skills of the various groups of people who will be using the system, as well as the frequency and intensity of usage. We can then define the task precisely and break it down into its constituent procedures and subtasks.

Information provided by our analyses of the task and the users enables us to allocate the work between the user and the machine. From it, specifications can also be drawn up for the individual component of the computer system. The object at this stage is to map subtasks onto **potential software tools** such as editors, programming languages, simulation aids, etc. (see Fig. 1.7).

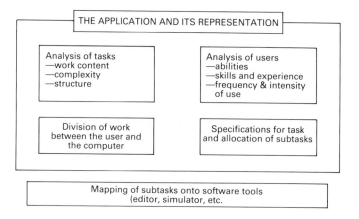

Fig. 1.7 — Defining and drawing up specifications for the application and its representation.

We are now in a position to determine the data objects for each software tool. The data objects may enter into a variety of relations with each other, from which we can set up the types of data structures required. To do this, we must first establish the attributes of the individual data objects.

The first step is to specify the basic (or generic) functions of the data objects and their attributes, including possible compound functions. We then determine the relations between the various data objects, attributes and functions. The results of this stage are the **input–output parameters** (commands, arguments, context, status variables) for each **software tool** (see Fig. 1.8).

Dialogues can be initiated by the computer, the user or both (i.e. hybrid). With this in mind we choose a suitable form of dialogue (transaction code, command language, menu, screen display with fixed fields, icons and pointers, natural language, etc.). Our decision is informed by the com-

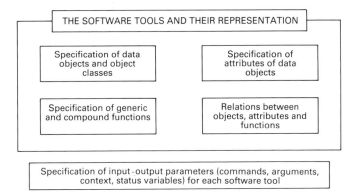

Fig. 1.8 — Defining and drawing up specifications for the software tools and their representation.

plexity, the steps required in the dialogue and the syntax. From this emerge the specifications for the **language structure** of our interface (Fig. 1.9).

There are various ways of handling input and output for interactive systems, based on speech, text, graphics, etc. Having established the most suitable form for our needs, we can choose the appropriate input–output devices (e.g. keyboard, screen monitor or pointer). We must decide how our information is to be organised (screen windows, screen pages, fixed fields, scrolling, etc.) and, finally, what forms it will take (i.e. the titles and terms to use in our display, symbols, highlighting techniques, etc.). This gives us the specifications for our **physical interface** (see Fig. 1.10).

1.4 SOFTWARE TOOLS

From a software engineering point of view, there are distinct advantages in using layered architectures (Fig. 1.11) for user interfaces. Shakel [8] reviews some of the currently available software tools for implementing user interfaces. Such tools enable interfaces to be designed more efficiently, and the quality of the end product is ergonomically superior.

In the following, we list each software implementation tool under the layer to which it belongs:

Input–output layer:

— input–output handler
— window system, display manager, picture manager
— graphics package (e.g. GKS, Quick-Draw).

Dialogue layer:

— dialogue manager
— menu and screen form manager (for text menus, screen forms, picture menus)

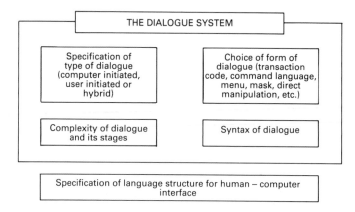

Fig. 1.9 — Defining and drawing up specifications for the dialogue system.

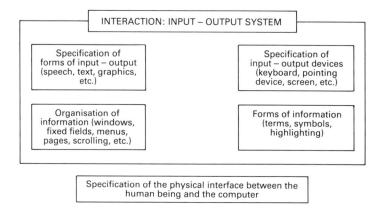

Fig. 1.10 — The input–output system.

— scanner (for segmenting input sequences into symbolic units)
— parsers for the syntactic analysis of input.

Application and task layer
— interpreter or compiler for status transition networks
— environment manager, tool manager, shell.

Commercially available products such as GEM [9] and the Apple Macintosh Toolbox [10] support largely low-level input–output dialogue within the confines of a fixed conceptual model (the interface is oriented to

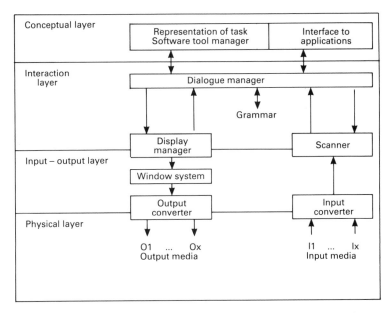

Fig. 1.11 — Some components of layered software architecture for user interfaces.

data objects and uses icons and pointers). Command language interfaces and general dialogue management are not supported. The GEM environment (Fig. 1.12) includes a convenient resource editor for setting up

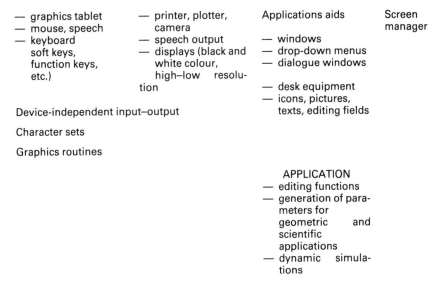

Fig. 1.12 — Graphics environment manager (GEM).

dialogue boxes, menu lists, screen displays (forms) and pictures. These tools enable the input–output interface to be relatively independent of specific input–output systems. Both GEM and LISA were used to implement the systems described below (in section 1.5).

Given the current lack of high-level systems, the user–programmer can develop his own tools by using 'metatools' such as compiler–compilers or programming environments from artificial intelligence (e.g. expert system shells). We adopted this approach in the system described below (section 1.5). For this the following metatools were created:

— a compiler for transition networks to represent tasks and dialogues
— a shell for a rule-based expert system

Apart from these, most of the components outlined above were implemented with a convenient system for creating windows. Fig. 1.13 illustrates a

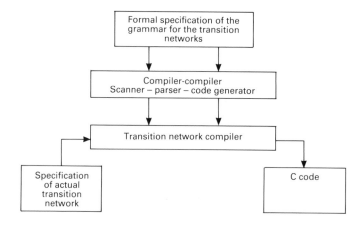

Fig. 1.13 — The use of compiler-compiler techniques.

compiler which was generated using compiler–compiler techniques and which translates the formal specifications for the task and dialogue representations (transition networks) into an executable C program.

Fig. 1.14 shows the structure of a shell for a rule-based diagnosis system in which the knowledge representation mechanism was implemented in a similar way to a production system. For the shell, an interpreter was written which allowed the development system to test the diagnosis system. A compiler produced executable C code for the target machine tool control system.

1.5 COMPUTER-INTEGRATED MANUFACTURING

The following project was concerned with developing certain systems for numeric control programming applications:

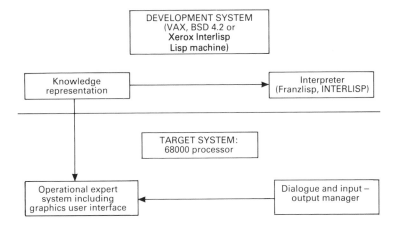

Fig. 1.14 — Expert system shell for diagnosing errors in numeric control machines.

— a new generation of graphically interactive dialogue processors for engineering applications (turning, milling, pressing and grinding)
— a production control system
— an expert system for error diagnosis in machine tools

Figs. 1.15 and 1.16 illustrate an advanced system for direct manipulation

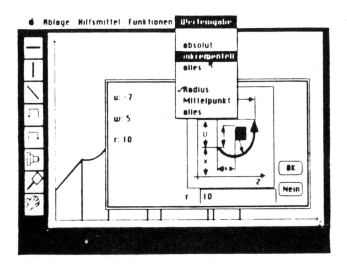

Fig. 1.15 — Programming for a turning operation.

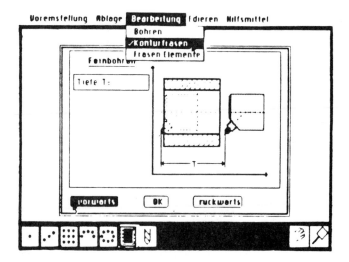

Fig. 1.16 — Programming for a milling operation.

of the screen display which was implemented with the Macintosh Toolbox. The designers were particularly concerned that the interface would be consistent with different processing requirements (for different generic objects and functions).

A second project involved the development of a production control system (see Fig. 1.17). A key aim here was to use a PC as a local intelligent

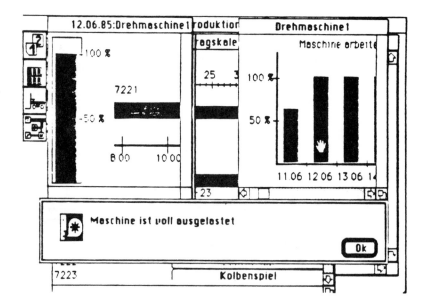

Fig. 1.17 — A production control system.

terminal, linked directly to a host computer and a central data base. This kind of configuration opens the door to fundamentally new forms of interaction in production control systems. The interface presented to the user information in a visual or symbolic form representing his working environment (i.e. office or workshop, etc.).

Fig. 1.18 shows part of a user interface for a system for diagnosing errors

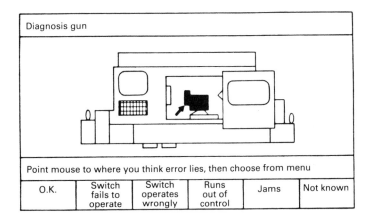

Fig. 1.18 — Expert system for diagnosing errors in numeric control machines.

in numeric control machines. By positioning a pointer in a picture or pressing soft keys, the user indicates where he thinks the error may lie and the computer gives possible causes. The system was written in OPS5 and Franzlisp [11] and implemented for the target system with a specially developed compiler written in C. Up to 40 000 possible error states are recognised.

All the above systems have been designed to achieve the most efficient possible interaction between the user and the system. The time needed in learning how to use the system has also been kept to a minimum. Because of this highly ergonomic approach, planning and programming can be carried out close to the actual machines on the factory floor. It also means that new technology and information systems can be introduced as smoothly and rapidly as possible.

REFERENCES

[1] Hayes, P. J. and Szekely, P. A. (1983) Graceful interaction through the COUSIN command interface. *Carnegie–Mellon University Computer Science Report CMU-CS-83-102.*

[2] Hayes, P. J., Szekely, P. A. and Lerner, R. A. (1985) Design alternatives for user interface management systems based on exper-

ience with COUSIN. *Proceedings of CHI '85, San Francisco, CA* pp. 169–175.

[3]   Stelovsky, J. (1984) XS-2: The user interface of an interactive system. *Dissertation*, ETH, Zurich.

[4]   Coutaz, J. (1984) A paradigm for user interface architecture. *Carnegie- -Mellon University Computer Science Report CMU-CS-84-124.*

[5]   Moran, T. P. (1981) The command language grammar: a representation for the user interface of interactive computer systems. *Int. J. Man–Machine Studies* **15** 3–50.

[6]   Card, S. K., Moran, T. P. and Newell, A. (1983) *The Psychology of Human–Computer Interaction*, Lawrence Erlbaum Associates, Hillsdale, New Jersey.

[7]   Fähnrich, K. P. and Kärcher, M. (1985) Software-Architekturen für Mensch-Computer-Schnittstellen — dargestellt am Beispiel eines multiligualen Textsystems. In: *Proceedings of Software Ergonomics Conference, 1985*, Teubner, Stuttgart.

[8]   Shakel, B. (ed.) (1985) *Proceedings of the NATO Workshop on Research Needs in Human–Computer Interaction, Loughborough.*

[9]   Miller, M. J. (1985) Digital Research's Graphics Environment Manager (GEM). *Popular Computing* **14**(5) 19–20.

[10] Williams, G. (1983) The LISA computer system. *Byte* **8**(2) 33.

[11] Anonymous (1984) AI language programs: expert systems under VAX/VMS computers. *Design* **23**(14) 239.

2

How to design dialogue systems for large computer applications

K.-P. Fähnrich

2.1 OUTLINE SPECIFICATIONS FOR A DIALOGUE SYSTEM

After a project has been accepted by the management, outline specifications for the system are drawn up (see Fig. 2.1). These should contain the

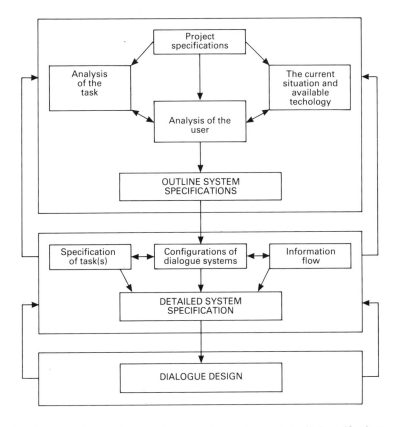

Fig. 2.1 — Designing a large application system: outline and detailed specifications.

following:

— an analysis of the task
— an analysis of the needs of the user
— an analysis of the current situation in the company and the technology available

As a rule the outline specifications should be produced jointly by departmental representatives, data processing experts and administrative staff. If necessary, communications specialists should also be involved.

2.1.1 Analysing the task

Standard methods of data processing and office management are used (a) to determine the structure and the flow of work and information and (b) to decide how the data base is to be organised. Representatives of those departments in the company which will actually use the output of the computer sytem must be directly involved in this process. When the analysis is completed, it must be decided whether to preserve existing work flows or, in the light of the projected data processing system, to go for a complete reorganisation of the company and its methods.

The design of the dialogue interface will be determined by certain features of the task itself:

— the complexity of the task
— whether it is closed or open ended
— its scope
— its structure

Simple dialogues, for instance, consist of a straightforward query. Complex dialogues can involve simulations of different production schedules. We shall define a task as **closed** if it consists of a repetition of single steps which can be reduced to an algorithm. Computer-aided design (CAD), in contrast, is a good example of an **open ended** task. Illustrations of closed and open-ended tasks are given in Fig. 2.2. The scope of a task can vary from

		TASK STRUCTURE	
		Closed	Open ended
F R E Q U E N C Y	frequent	Test processing Inputting data Numeric control of machine tools	Scientific applications Programming Process control
	occasional	Bank terminal Information query systems Learning programs	Decision support systems Diagnostic systems Construction design support systems

Fig. 2.2 — Open-ended and closed tasks.

a few hours to weeks or even months. Thus, to produce a long and detailed data record describing a complicated engineering process can take several hours. Long dialogues need to be monitored more carefully and we must pay particular attention to the way in which the information is organised.

The structure of the task is important. Dialogues can be designed much more efficiently if data items are always input in a fixed sequence (an example is entering information for an invoice). In a transaction-oriented system for interactive order processing, however, the structure of the dialogue must reflect more closely the requirements of an interview. In most cases the sequence of transactions will have to be quite flexible.

Apart from the structure of the task itself, we also have to consider the external conditions under which the user may be performing it. These include distractions, time pressure, contacts with customers, etc. Conducting interactive dialogues under certain conditions (processing passengers in an airport, serving customers in a travel agents or at a bank counter, etc.) can be particularly difficult: members of the public can be in a hurry, nervous, upset and rude, especially if they have to wait a long time in a queue to be attended to. In such cases it is obviously better to take more trouble to design a short but effective dialogue (using action codes, mnemonic abbreviations, standard input formats, and so on). The user would also require intensive training, so that he is fully familiar with the system. If the user needs to use several different application programs alongside each other in the same system, it is important for the dialogue to be as standard as possible. This is preferable to having a different dialogue for each application, even though that might be better from a purely technical point of view. Key strokes, function codes and mnemonics which are specific to particular applications should be avoided.

It should be possible in future to offer the user a choice between different forms of dialogue depending on frequency of usage. For infrequent applications, the user would respond to prompts from the computer running a structurally complex but easy-to-use dialogue program. For frequent applications, however, a hybrid form of dialogue would be available, or even one in which interaction is entirely initiated by the human being. The outlay for implementing such systems would be higher, but could be offset by the use of dialogue generators.

2.1.2 Analysing the needs of the user

There is still a widespread lack of facilities for analysing the needs of the user. In this section we shall discuss what we consider to be the key factors involved, i.e. the skills and capabilities of the typical user and the frequency with which he accesses the system. Information about these factors enables us (a) to assess how to make most effective use of the system, (b) to estimate the outlay for training and (c) to decide provisionally what form of dialogue to use.

To analyse prospective user groups, we can start from the existing organisational structure of the company. This will allow us to divide tasks into, for example, support services (secretarial functions, text processing, etc.), administrative, technical or managerial. This will give us an early idea of the general capabilities of the main user groups (see Fig. 2.3). Job descriptions and other methods can be used to fill in the details (Fig. 2.4).

The information gained in this way indicates how the user may be expected to interact with the computer. He might assume one of the following roles:

(a) active role: the user initiates and controls access and enquiries to the system
(b) passive role: the system initiates and controls the interaction
(c) monitoring role: the user monitors external access to the system
(d) intermediary role: the user either helps others to access the system or accesses the computer himself on their behalf

We should also be aware of the abilities and skills of the user, i.e. (a) his intelligence, (b) his programming experience, (c) his previous experience with application systems and (d) any specialised training which he may have received. Frequency of access to the system may be classified as constant, from time to time, or seldom, etc.

The following guidelines — which are by no means exhaustive — may be useful in evaluating the information about the various user groups and their capabilities.

(a) Personnel providing support services can and should be given extensive training in how to see the computer system. The form of dialogue should be as powerful as possible and the user should be able to access the system easily. We should reckon with constant or frequent usage, and the role of the user should be of the active or intermediary type.
(b) The same goes for administrative tasks. Depending on the job, however, the user may access the system either from time to time or seldom. His role is largely passive, with external help or supervision on hand. Recent trends in organisation theory favour greater autonomy and independence for this kind of work, which would demand higher outlay in system design and staff training.
(c) Technical staff often have previous training in data processing and experience in using application systems. They can be expected to handle more difficult, complex and powerful dialogues and to adopt an active role in most cases. However, this is primarily true only where the application software is accessed very frequently. For less frequent operations we may expect the user to assume a more passive role, with interaction initiated by the computer.
(d) Managers and senior staff still obtain most of the information they want either directly or indirectly from third parties. If not, the form of the dialogue will have to be very carefully designed and its users assumed to have no previous training.
(e) User-initiated dialogues are feasible for those experienced in applications and programming, especially where it is important to have

MANAGERIAL TASKS	SPECIALIST TASKS
Lead and motivate Communicate Represent	Prepare reports Carry through projects Develop new methods
Subject or event oriented Self-initiative required Background knowledge essential	Project-oriented Self-initiative required within area Specialist knowledge essential

ADMINISTRATIVE TASKS	SUPPORT SERVICES
Procedural Handle (initial) contacts Provide documentation	Provide internal services Partly procedural

Procedure or event oriented
Organised
Specialist knowledge
  important
	Event oriented
	Externally initiated
	Specialist knowledge less
	  important

Fig. 2.3 — User groups.

MANAGERIAL TASKS	SPECIALIST TASKS	ADMINISTRATIVE TASKS	SUPPORT SERVICES

Entrepeneur
Sales manager
Chief buyer
Production
  manager
Board member
	Developmental
	  engineer
	Production
	  planner
	Foreman
	System analyst
	Legal staff
		Accountant
		Purchasing
		  clerk
		Bank teller
		Accounts clerk
		Store
		  controller
			Secretaries
			(Data) typists
			Messengers
			Telephonists
			Shorthand
			  typists

Fig. 2.4 — Examples of different types of user groups.

power and flexibility. Command languages, interpretive languages and interactive programming languages can all be used here to great effect.

(f) if the user is assumed to be of no more than average intelligence, with little or no experience of data processing or application software, then so-called hybrid or computer-initiated forms of dialogue are more appropriate. If these are not powerful enough for our purposes (e.g. an airline booking system accessed directly from the airport departure terminal), the users will need extensive training.

(g) Thorough training is very worthwhile if the system is used extensively. Tutorial data files help the user to access the system more efficiently and handle more powerful and complex forms of dialogue. The user's role will be either active or passive, depending on whether the task is open ended or closed.

(h) If accessed infrequently the system should be as user friendly as possible. This means that the dialogue should be self-explanatory, easy to learn and tolerant of input errors rather than powerful as such. Computer-initiated or hybrid forms of dialogue which do not need extensive input errors checking routines are superior here and should incorporate clear system messages and sophisticated support and help facilities. The user should be able to learn them quickly and future expansions should be based on natural forms of communictaion (e.g. icons and pointers or natural language systems).

(i) The dialogue interface and user training should be given a high priority in order to get the best out of the system.

(j) Manufacturers have already begun to pay more attention to dialogue systems (in the shape of user interface generators, help facilities, tutorial support, etc.). in the long term this should obviate the need for special training programmes.

2.1.3   Analysing the current situation and the available technology

The potential and the limitations of existing technology within a company should be examined at an early stage in the design of a new system. This means looking at the following:

— the capacity of central and local data processing systems
— existing network and information transfer systems
— existing local terminals and peripheral devices
— existing data bases
— existing application systems
— plans for long-term expansion

Links with other manufacturers and external suppliers (such as software houses) should be clarified. Updates on recent market developments should be obtained, as well as all available information on comparable systems.

2.1.4   The outline specification

The results of the various analyses are now converted into an outline system specification for discussion with the relevant technical and managerial staff. This process might have to be repeated several times. Only when the outline specification has been accepted by everyone involved should any further steps be taken. The author's experience of large-scale applications shows that this phase can take anything from three to six months to complete.

2.2   DETAILED SPECIFICATIONS FOR A DIALOGUE SYSTEM

The object at this stage is to map the outline specification onto individual tasks, to describe these in detail and to plan the control and flow of information. For this we must

— specify who will do what

— draw up information and work flow plans
— produce configurations for dialogue systems

There are various techniques for eliciting and representing information and for the evaluation of cost-benefit ratios, etc. (see [1]).

It is very important to distinguish between the system user and the terminal operator. These roles can be combined into a single person or they can be quite separate. The typical case is shown in configuration (a) in Fig. 2.5, where the system user and the terminal operator are identical. This is

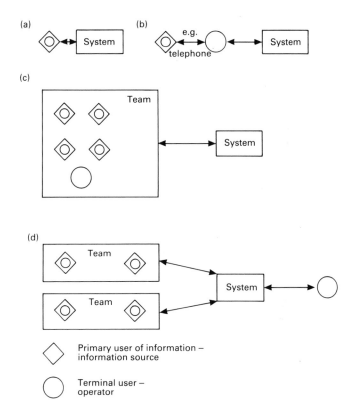

Fig. 2.5 — Configurations for dialogue systems I (see Martin [2]).

actually preferred in modern organisation theory — at least for routine administrative applications.

In configuration (b) an 'operator' has been interposed between the system user and the terminal operator. This arrangement is suitable where a manager in a company accesses the computer system only through his secretary or assistant. The current trend, however, is for the user of the information provided by the system to be less and less dependent on the terminal operator. Managers, for example, want access to information outside normal working hours and, on the whole, prefer to have greater flexibility.

In configuration (c) the user frequently consults the computer and prefers to access the system himself. Only in exceptional cases and for difficult transactions does he involve a trained and experienced terminal operator. The operator might happen to be a member of a particular team or section in the company (e.g. sales, invoice processing) or he might act as terminal operator for several teams at once (as in configuration (d)).

In (c) and (d) the trained operator may not just be there to help other users (the role of intermediary): he is their immediate supervisor. In other words he is on hand to ensure that the security of data is preserved, to prevent overbookings in seat reservation systems, or check the consistency of data records for a stock control system. These functions will be supported by appropriate software modules and it will be mandatory to summon the operator when things go wrong.

On-line centres, terminal control rooms and information distribution centres are found in large-scale interactive data processing systems with possibly several hundred terminals. Complex structures are required for handling the flow of work and information. In configuration (e) (Fig. 2.6)

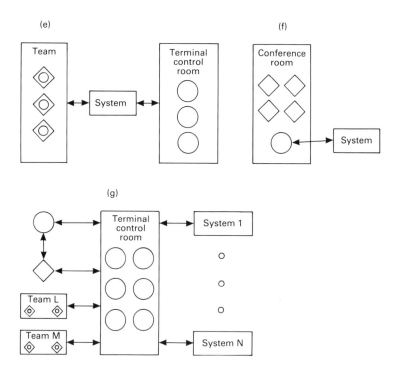

Fig. 2.6 — Configurations for dialogue systems II (see Martin [2]).

the team is supported by a terminal control room. Real-time processing, which is especially demanding on the computer, often needs to be backed up by the following measures:

(a) engagement of less highly trained personnel to correct data input errors
(b) special provision for protecting data and ensuring data security (system maintenance)
(c) intervention by the operator should certain limits be exceeded (e.g. overbookings, negative stock inventories, overloading of production line)
(d) modification of input parameters for automatic real-time systems

Configuration (f) can be used in conferences. The trained terminal operator simulates the effects of decisions (e.g. on stocks and raw materials held, timetables, projected costs).

Configuration (g) is very complex and combines most of the arrangements discussed above. In addition, several data processing systems are in operation at the same time.

A number of factors must be borne in mind when evaluating different configurations.

(a) Centralised data processing systems (e.g. run from terminal control rooms) can handle much heavier processing loads, with trained operators fully exploiting the greater power of the facilities available. The operators can be expected to run powerful application programs with more complicated and versatile dialogue interfaces as well as providing support and training for less qualified staff. A centralised data processing system is often ideal where the primary users of the information are either unwilling or unable to make full use of the system on their own (e.g. for management information systems or for conferences).
(b) Decentralised data processing systems are more flexible and can often be introduced with less disruption to the existing organisation of a company. As we have already pointed out, there is a trend in routine administrative applications towards on-the-spot transactions. Because of rapidly falling hardware costs, local intelligent systems are becoming more and more attractive, a trend which is being reinforced by the increased use of PCs as workstations in clusters or local area networks. We are also seeing improved forms of dialogue, in the shape of icons and pointers, help facilities and tutorial software.
(c) Large interactive systems (e.g. for banks, insurance companies, building societies, mail order firms) may have several hundred or even thousand terminals accessing correspondingly large and complex data bases. For the foreseeable future these will be implemented as a mixture of centralised and local processing. We are likely to see greater integration of office communications with traditional data processing applications. While communication in the office tends, by its very nature, to be local, other functions (such as archiving, backing-up files

and cost-intensive tasks such as photosetting, laser printing and scanning) will continue to be centralised.

Detailed specifications for an interactive system must be carefully studied by everyone in the company who will be affected by data processing. The consultation process may have to be repeated more than once and cost effectiveness will play a major part in the evaluation. For a large application system, it may take from six months to a year to reach a decision.

2.3 DIALOGUE DESIGN

2.3.1 Procedure
From the point of view of the end user, the most important decisions are made during this stage (see Fig. 2.7). if the above procedure has been

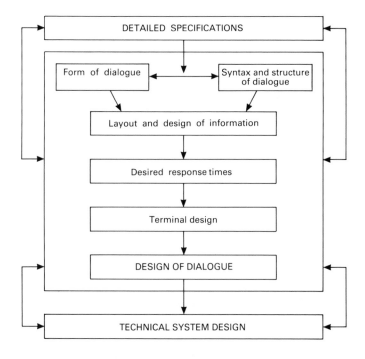

Fig. 2.7 — Designing dialogues for large application systems.

followed, enough information will be available to decide on a form of dialogue (or, perhaps, a mixture of different forms) which will both do the job and satisfy the user. Once again there is paucity of standard tools and resources (e.g. decision tables) in this area. Fig. 2.8 shows the procedure to follow in the design of a dialogue interface.

2.3.2   Forms of dialogue and design techniques

Depending on the role which the user is to play in the system as a whole, we distinguish between computer-initiated, user-initiated and hybrid forms of dialogue (see Fig. 2.9 and Chapter 1, section 1.3). Fig. 2.10 summarises the advantages and disadvantages of user-initiated dialogues. If the dialogue is initiated and controlled by the computer, the user is presented with a fixed set of choices at each stage in the interaction) see Fig. 2.11 for a comparison of the advantages and disadvantages). In hybrid dialogues the initiative shifts between the user and the system.

In most large systems where numerous terminals are controlled by a central host computer, we can also note the following characteristics.

(a) In a user-initiated dialogue the user initiates the first transaction.
(b) In a computer-initiated dialogue the first transaction is initiated by the system itself.

We take a transaction to refer to an exchange of information between the user and the system (in either direction).

During the last ten years user-initiated dialogues have tended to be seen as lacking in 'user friendliness'. On this we should note the following points.

(a) To date no-one has yet given a precise definition of what 'user friendliness' really is (although the German Standards Institute has begun work on this question [3]). Categorical statements of this kind have therefore little value.
(b) There is no single form of dialogue which is superior to all the rest. The system designer must take into account all the relevant factors, many of which will work directly against each other (the nature of the task, the user profile, the limits of the available technology, the cost effectiveness of the project as a whole, etc.).

Ease of use and learning time are important criteria in the choice of a form of dialogue. Fig. 2.12 shows comparative learning times for different systems. The quality of the system design, however, can produce considerable variations on the mean values given in Fig. 2.12. A secretary, for instance, can learn how to use the main functions of some text processing systems in a couple of hours: for other systems, she may need several weeks to achieve proper mastery. If the user is looking for both power and flexibility, he should choose a form of dialogue on the left-hand side of Fig. 2.12. If flexibility and efficiency are less important than ease of use and learnability, he would be better advised to choose one from the right-hand side.

Forms of dialogue which are easy to use often make quite heavy demands

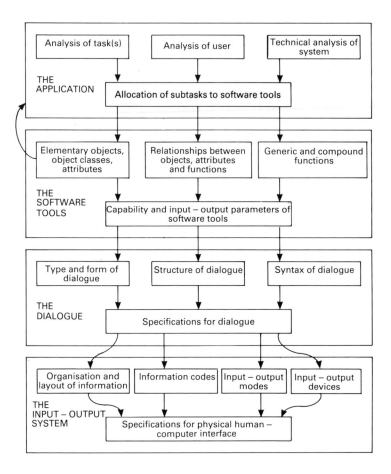

Fig. 2.8 — Designing a dialogue interface.

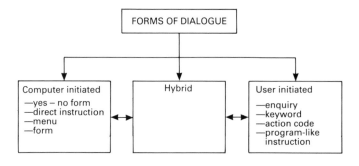

Fig. 2.9 — Forms of dialogue (from Haubner).

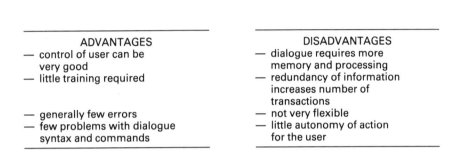

ADVANTAGES	DISADVANTAGES
— Lower costs of transmission	— more difficult (demands on recall and recognition memory)
— precise and efficient language of communication	— takes longer to learn
— very flexible: user controls course of dialogue	— greater risk of mistakes: requires complex error checks

Fig. 2.10 — Advantages and disadvantages of user-initiated dialogues.

ADVANTAGES	DISADVANTAGES
— control of user can be very good	— dialogue requires more memory and processing
— little training required	— redundancy of information increases number of transactions
— generally few errors	— not very flexible
— few problems with dialogue syntax and commands	— little autonomy of action for the user

Fig. 2.11 — Advantages and disadvantages of computer-initiated dialogues.

on a network and so cost more to run. Intelligent subsystems are more suitable in such cases.

Another factor in evaluating a dialogue interface is the information bandwidth, which can vary for each system. This is not necessarily proportional to the telecommunications bandwidth of the terminal lines, since it can be significantly increased with different coding.

The information bandwidth indicates the speed at which information can be transmitted in a particular dialogue system. Fig. 2.13 shows various types of dialogue in relation to their information bandwidth and how easy they are to learn and use. The information bandwidth depends very much on the application and can only be roughly estimated.

The comparison clearly shows that forms of dialogue which make use of symbolic or pictorial representations have major advantages. However, the technical outlay required to implement them is quite high, which can make text-based interfaces more cost effective.

In choosing a particular form of dialogue, one important factor must be taken into account, namely the degree of flexibility required. Job control languages, for example, can be extremely versatile in their application, especially when combined with facilities for controlling program execution (e.g. variables, labels, jumps, macros). As a general rule we can say that, the more difficult a dialogue is to learn and use, the more flexible it is.

(a) A form of dialogue which is easy to use is generally designed for a single fixed application. It cannot normally be transferred to other applications without adaptation.

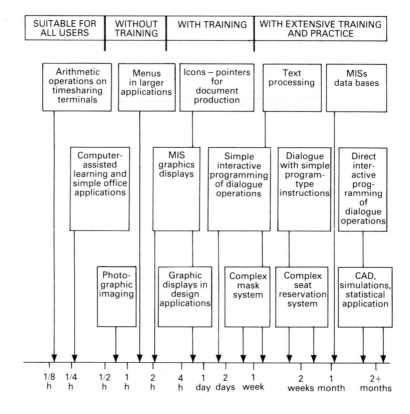

Fig. 2.12 — Illustration of how easy different forms of dialogue are to use, as measured by the time required to learn them (MIS = management information system).

(b) Forms of dialogue based on job control languages or programming-type languages are more difficult to learn but have more universal application. For a large number of applications, it is worth the initial effort.

(c) At the other end of the extreme, we have the manager type of dialogue, which is designed to be largely self-explanatory. Normally equipped with graphics and symbols, it should combine high information bandwidths with ease of usage and learnability.

Icons and pointers can provide enough flexibility to be considered a hybrid form of dialogue. We shall discuss these in detail below.

2.3.2.1 Well-established techniques of dialogue design

At this point we shall compare the characteristics of particular forms of dialogue and review their advantages and disadvantages.

User-initiated forms of dialogue can use the following techniques:

(a) simple query.

(b) mnemonic transaction codes

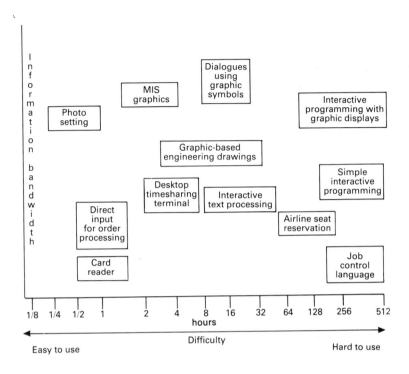

Fig. 2.13 — Comparison of information bandwidth and difficulty for different forms of dialogue (MIS, management information system).

(c) natural language
(d) programming-type instructions

For a simple query, an input by the user results in the desired information's being output. In simple commercial information systems this is quite adequate. The technique has the advantage of being efficient and cheap to implement. The disadvantages are that it has a rather limited range of application and that the occasional user has to learn and remember the proper vocabulary to frame enquiries.

For (b), inputs are made up of action codes and optional function codes defining parameters and their values. Mnemonic abbreviations make the codes easier to handle. This form of dialogue is especially suited to on-line booking systems, such as for airlines. Compared with (a), it makes more demands on human memory and requires more training (including follow-up courses). Its advantage is that it is very efficient.

Dialogues for search systems, personnel and management information systems and data base enquiry systems tend to base their interaction on natural language (type (c) above). Each alphanumeric input parameter is preceded by a unique natural language key word. This allows a relatively normal conversation to take place between the user and the computer, although there is a danger of lexical ambiguities.

Type (d) dialogues are found in data base enquiry languages, interactive statistical and graphics packages, planning and simulation systems. They show many similarities to interactive programming languages and combine power with flexibility. Although easier to learn than standard programming languages, they are more difficult to master than the previous techniques. The main drawback is that they presuppose a certain competence in computer programming, so they are not suitable for the occasional user.

We now turn our attention to three typical computer-initiated forms of dialogue:

(a) instructions or messages issued to the user (either singly or at once)
(b) menus
(c) form input

In type (a), an exchange takes place between the computer, which issues instructions or asks questions, and the user, who responds to these questions. Questions can be presented one at a time or all at once in a single frame. Examples are customer information systems and infrequently used booking systems. This form of dialogue has considerable advantages for occasional users: the computer controls the interaction in a way that is clear to the user, inputs are checked for validity, and on-line help facilities are generally available. However, because of the way the information is organised and sequentially output, such systems are not particularly flexible or powerful.

Menu-based forms of dialogue are in widespread use. The principle of the menu is simple enough. From a relatively short list of possible responses, the user chooses one. A screen can display several lists at a time, or a single list can extend across several screen pages. Menu-based systems are easily learned and the user is clearly guided through them. This can be a disadvantage to a frequent and experienced user, however, who may feel the system is too restricted and inflexible. The field of application is also limited, because both the processing steps and the information have to be structured as a tree.

Menus are often combined with screen forms which contain fields for input from the user. Both menus and screen forms are used for accessing customer master data files and data bases, etc. The advantages are that the information is well presented and such systems are easily learned. Possible drawbacks include minimal requirements for peripheral devices and the need for sufficiently powerful hardware.

2.3.2.2 Designing hybrid dialogues

Until now we have presented largely well-established and conventional forms of dialogue. During the last few years, however, hybrid forms of dialogue have become very important. We shall discuss the currently most significant representatives of this type, i.e. those which use icons and pointers in the direct manipulation of screen contents.

2.3.2.2.1 Icons and pointers

The basic idea of icons and pointers is to represent on screen the working environment and its objects in symbolic form. Such systems are usually implemented on modern workstations. Each station is equipped with a high resolution screen in which the information displayed corresponds, pixel by pixel, to bits held in main memory (so-called bit mapping). The screen is used in conjunction with a pointing device (e.g. mouse, joystick or touch-sensitive surface).

The interface displays a fixed and limited conceptual model of the particular application area. In practice, the suitability of this form of dialogue depends largely on the appropriateness of the model and how accurately it reflects the objects, functions and relationships of the working environment it is supposed to depict. The model must be clear and comprehensible to the user.

In a typical dialogue based on icons and pointers, the user performs rapid, step-by-step operations with his device which have an immediate effect on the objects displayed on the screen. Windows are often used to represent different parts of the working environment and even an inexperienced user should have little difficulty in learning a small number of powerful operations which, within a small and well-defined area, can be applied universally. For this reason, icons and pointers are mainly suitable for non-specialist or occasional users of data processing.

2.3.2.2.2 Natural language

The most important medium of human communication is undoubtedly natural language, for which we can find numerous possible applications in human–computer interfaces. Some of these are as follows:

(a) question-and-answer dialogues and communication with expert systems
(b) setting up and interrogating data bases
(c) programming
(d) automatic translation
(e) Linguistic text processing, e.g. automatic spelling checks, checking for textual consistency, summaries, text searches and text generation
(f) combined natural language and graphics systems

The technical and financial outlay required to implement even a quite modest natural language interface is very large.

The naturalness of human language is generally advanced as a good reason for its use in man–machine interfaces. Because everyone can use language, there is no need for the user to master a new and difficult formal system of communication. Natural language has already evolved into an efficient tool for referring to objects, events and abstract entities in the world around us. It is also argued that natural language would make computers more widely available to many more users. Even 'professional' users would find life easier, because they would no longer have the problem of translating users' requirements into the terms and concepts of an artificial language.

We must not overlook the fact that natural language interfaces are beset by major difficulties. The most natural means of communication between human beings is not necessarily the most natural medium for man and the computer. Many properties of natural language are not yet understood and have certainly not been reduced to formal algorithms. Implemented natural language systems encompass, at best, a limited fragment of normal language and, even then, are restricted to particular applications and subject areas. There is the ever-present danger that the user — under the illusion that the computer really understands normal language — will have exaggerated expectations of the capabilities of the system. This can lead to frustration, wrong interpretations and mistakes based on semantic over-generalisations (so-called semantic overshoot). In an implemented natural language interface, it is most important that the user is at all times very clear about what the system can actually do and that each transaction is verified.

2.3.2.3   Symbiotic forms of dialogue

The dialogue interfaces described in previous sections all have their advantages and disadvantages. Recent attention, however, has focused on a relatively new development, i.e. so-called symbiotic dialogues. These are intended to combine three types of communication, namely natural language, icons and pointers, and formal language, into a single common representation (see Fig. 2.14).

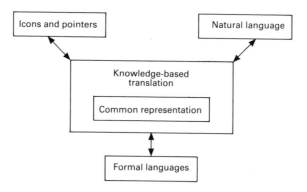

Fig. 2.14 — Proposal for a symbiotic dialogue interface.

The various types of communication are brought together in such a way that they are changed and adapted to suit the needs of the user and his context. This can only be done given the right technology and if the application, together with the information which is being input and output, is suitable in the first place. Furthermore, the system must have enough inbuilt knowledge and intelligence to handle complex dialogues and to do the necessary adaptive processing.

A symbiotic dialogue system would have the following advantages.

(a) If the interface could handle different forms of communication at the same time, we would be able to introduce a degree of redundancy into the input and output. This would prevent misunderstanding and avoid the need for corrections and corroborative enquiries.
(b) We could compensate for the known deficiencies of certain types of communication (such as the limitations of icons and pointers in providing programmable input parameters) by bringing in elements of other types.

Fig. 2.15 shows how a symbiotic dialogue interface combining natural language and graphics could access a data base and output the results.

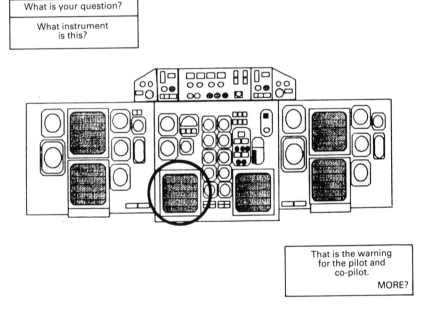

Fig. 2.15 — Integration of natural language and graphics based dialogues.

2.3.3   The structure and syntax of the dialogue

To converse with a computer we must be able to perform certain control operations. For example, the user must be able to open and close the dialogue when he wants to. In confused or difficult situations the user should be able to turn to the system for help on how to continue. He should be able not only to interrupt the dialogue but also to resume it when he wants to.

These operations, or transactions, are largely independent of any particular application and should be an integral part of any standard dialogue interface. They should also be simple enough for the occasional or inexperienced user.

2.3.3.1   Initialisation or opening procedure
The computer always begins with a prompt from the system to the user. in large data processing systems the opening procedure is in two stages:

(a) the user inputs his password
(b) the user selects his application (runs a program)

In many commercial systems stage (b) is menu driven.

2.3.3.2   Help in a dialogue
The help key is very important for the inexperienced or occasional user. It should always be available. If at all possible, it should not destroy the information built up on the screen. The user should be able to summon help to varying degrees of detail and error messages should obviously correspond as far as possible to the available help information.

The user should be able to interrupt complex dialogues either after or during each transaction. This is important if, for example

(a) the user wishes to end a dialogue prematurely (he does not want any more information)
(b) the user wants to preserve the status of a dialogue because he has to leave the terminal for a certain period
(c) the user wishes to interrupt the main dialogue temporarily while he searches for information elsewhere by conducting a secondary dialogue
(d) the user must do something else on the computer at the request, say, of a customer or colleagues

The software module which handles the interruption should give the user various options — possibly in menu form. The main ones are as follows:

(a) store the status of the current transaction and return to it later
(b) return to the current dialogue from the point of detachment
(c) break off the dialogue altogether
(d) display the status of the dialogue and the host system
(e) skip forward to another point in the dialogue
(f) log off from the host system

The undo key allows the user to retrace one or more steps in the dialogue. This function is of tremendous value for learning how to use the system. It is, however, quite difficult to implement in many data base systems and takes up extra memory. For complex dialogues, it is helpful to be able to define specific points to which the user may return if he makes a mistake or just wants to see the effects of a series of inputs.

So far we have tried to give some idea of the structure of different forms of dialogue. The syntax of a dialogue is to some extent dependent on the particular application. The syntax can be extremely complicated (as, for instance, in programming languages), or very basic (as in dialogues which rely on icons and pointers). The syntax of form-based dialogue interfaces will be discussed in the next chapter, where we shall also consider how to organise our information on the screen.

While the planned response times for a system may well be influenced by such issues as cost effectiveness and processing requirements, the main criterion should be what is pyschologically best for the user in interaction with the machine. The following factors must therefore be borne in mind.

(a) Response time expectations: we should aim for a maximum average response time of 2 s.
(b) The various stages of a task: the user will want to complete each stage as quickly as possible. Longer response times are permissible towards the end of a stage, otherwise they should be as short as possible.
(c) Properties of short-term memory: human short-term memory is comparatively limited, so prolonged response times result in memory lapses or even corruption of the information which the user is trying to retain.

Fig. 2.16 lists typical response times for large interactive systems with

Dialogue operation	Maximum system response time (s)
Response to control commands	0.1
Initialisation of system	3.0
Requests for service routines	
Simple	2.0
Complex	5.0
Load and activate	15–60
Error message	2–4
Response to user identification	2
Information about next step	<5
Response to simple listing query	2
Response to simple status query	2
Response to complex query in tabular form	2–4
Get next page–frame	0.5–1
Response to command to perform processing operation	<15
Light pen input	1
Drawing with light pen input	0.1
Response to complex query in graphics representation	2–10
Response to graphics manipulation	2
Response to intervention by user in automatic processes	4

Fig. 2.16 — System response times in relation to specific dialogue operations (see Martin [2]).

several hundred or more users. With intelligent subsystems, these times can be much faster.

2.4   SYSTEM DESIGN

In this section we shall only touch on the technical aspects of designing a data processing system (see Fig. 2.17). Our form of dialogue will be heavily

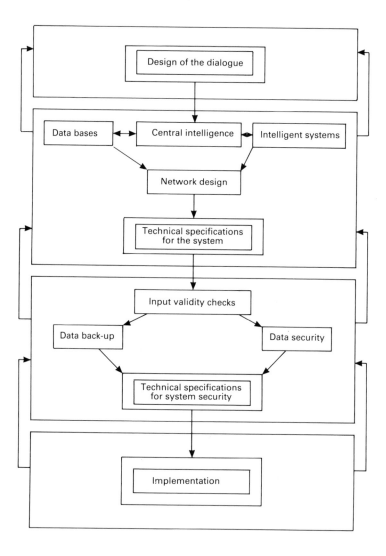

Fig. 2.17 — Designing a large application system with security in mind.

influenced by the decision either to centralise all processing at a host computer or to opt for intelligent subsystems, local work stations or even personal computers. The long-term trend increasingly favours decentralised processing activities.

Intelligent subsystems have considerable advantages. Some activities can be performed off line, and reserve stations can substitute for host computer terminals which are out of action. The work can be organised during the down periods so that no transactions are lost and none of the data files is damaged by errors or warm restarts. The next ten years will see a move towards combined central and local processing according to the requirements of a particular company. One problem which has still not been satisfactorily solved is how to preserve the consistency of distributed data bank systems with on-line access.

2.5 SECURITY

Preserving the security of data is becoming more and more important as increasing amounts of personal, classified and commercial data are stored in data files directly accessible via terminals. It is vital to ensure that unauthorised persons cannot get at such data and that the system itself is able to pick up and deal with any violations.

All forms of protection against the unlawful use of data and programs are based on the system's identifying the terminal or its user before it decides on the type of access to allow. Security is especially important in large on-line data processing systems, where workflow and processing needs will determine who has access to which data and programs. When a user (or terminal) identifies himself, special software checks through hierarchies of passwords are made to decide what sort of access can be granted. The system designer should be aware that data protection must be supported by surveillance mechanisms. These ensure that the system reacts to violations and, if necessary, reports them to the staff responsible.

The syntax of the dialogue should be designed to minimise the risk of input mistakes on the part of the user. Mistakes should be picked up with validity checks, which are easy to implement in computer-initiated dialogues.

Backing-up of data is usually a matter of organisation and should not be neglected, since the user of a large on-line systems relies heavily on his data and programs being available when he needs them.

2.6 IMPLEMENTATION

At this stage in the design of a system, it is a good idea to simulate the dialogue with prospective users (see Fig. 2.18).

Programmers are often surprised at users' reactions to the dialogues they have designed and written. Operations which are obvious to them are often confusing to the user. Before final programming begins, the system designer should develop alternative dialogue strategies and simulate them with the

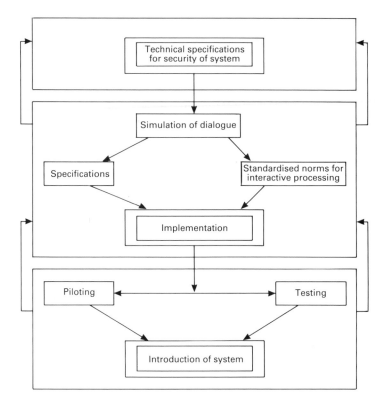

Fig. 2.18 — Implementing and introducing a large application system.

user. Software for simulating interactive transactions is available. The structure of the dialogue can be modified and refined during the simulation itself and user's reactions can be recorded and statistically analysed.

The advantage of simulators is that the dialogue can be altered while the project is still in the experimental stage. As soon as the potential user is thoroughly familar with the system, he will be able to pick up any deficiencies and misleading elements in the dialogue and suggest improvements.

At this stage it is possible to draw up specifications for developing a data processing system. The designers should examine the possibility of using suitable dialogue generators (for masks, menus and windows) and define general standards for interactive processing which might also be extended to existing applications. When all this is done — and not before — the system itself can be implemented.

2.7 INTRODUCING THE SYSTEM

There is a large body of reference material in the field of organisation and methods and systems analysis which is relevant to the introduction of a data processing system (see [1]). Whichever approach is adopted, it is useful to set up and evaluate a pilot system before installing the main system itself.

REFERNECES

[1] Becker, M., Haberfellner, R. and Liebetrau, G. (1988) *Electronic Data Processing in Practice,* Ellis Horwood, Chichester.
[2] Martin, J. (1972) *Design of Man–Computer Dialogues,* Prentice-Hall, Englewood Cliffs, New Jersey.
[3] German Standards Institute (1984) *DIN 66234.*

3

Information design for screens and screen menus

J. Ziegler

3.1 SCREEN DISPLAYS IN HUMAN–COMPUTER INTERACTION

Screen displays (often referred to as 'screens') are found in all interactive applications. They are, however, especially popular in commercial data processing and data base management systems.

We shall concentrate below on the design and layout of information for VDU screens, with particular reference to character-oriented screens and data processing transactions. The basic principles, however, are universal and should also apply to most other systems (such as desk-top PCs with raster screens).

Communication between the user and the computer takes place at four different levels:

(a) task level: this concerns the type, extent and structure of the task
(b) functional level: this refers to the data objects and software functions
(c) dialogue level: this is concerned with the steps or stages of the dialogue and the command structure
(d) level of interaction: we are concerned here with how the information is coded, represented and technically implemented

The level of interaction is that part of the interface which is directly visible to the user. All the other levels can only contribute to the communication if the user himself already has some concept of them: this concept might be based on previous experience of computers or might evolve during the course of communication over a period of time. Thus, for instance, a menu displayed on the screen only has any meaning for the user if he already knows (or can deduce form the menu itself) the fact that it offers him a series of alternative commands which he can send to the system.

To make real use of the system, however, the user must also be aware of what data items and software functions are available to him and what role they play in the processing task as a whole. Thus, a menu option, 'Account status', will refer to certain data items on which operations (e.g. 'Change the contents of the account') can be performed: such an operation will be carried out at the functional level in the light of a known objective at the task level.

In this chapter we are mainly concerned with designing and organising information at the level of interaction. We shall pay particular attention to the following issues:

(a) the principles of visual perception
(b) the visual design of screen output
(c) the best ways of coding information on screen

Information design and layout in screen output is often markedly inferior to what is usually found in standard paper forms (which tend not to be models of user friendliness themselves). Despite this, both users and designers of systems hardly seem to be aware of the potential for improvement. Software developers will put forward a whole series of arguments for not improving the ergonomics of their products. Dismissing software ergonomics as 'pure cosmetics' and placing functionality before user friendliness, they will refer to the high level of competence usually found in the in-house user or stress the prohibitive cost of improving and standardising an application system with a long history of development behind it. From a purely ergonomic standpoint, however, we should emphasise the following points.

(a) As soon as the user sees material on his screen, he structures it. Well-structured material reduces unnecessary search times and the frequency of mistakes. It also increases learning speed and the user's acceptance of the system.
(b) Both new and experienced users must have ready access to visual help facilities (e.g. to correct mistakes or to change what has been done).
(c) The cost of producing ergonomic packages and programs is not excessive if interfaces are developed with suitable software tools (e.g. generators for screens, menus and dialogues).
(d) If we apply ergonomic standards for the design and layout of information to as many data processing operations as possible within a company, we will have a much improved and more consistent system of communication.

3.2 THE IMPORTANCE OF SCREEN DISPLAYS

Screen displays allow us to formalise and structure the input and output of information. Fig. 3.1 is an example of a screen display.

Varying degrees of interaction are possible with screens, depending on when the computer reacts to input. We can distinguish three levels of interaction. Presented in order of increasing degrees of interaction, these are as follows.

(a) **Screen-oriented interaction**: the computer responds when the user has finished with the whole screen. We can also refer to this as **transaction oriented**.
(b) **Field-oriented interaction**: the computer responds when the user has input to each field.

```
Richard Meyer:              SAMPLE SALES RECORD           :Date    :01.02.84
              :        FOR ORDER PROCESSING DEPARTMENT   :User    :JK

Registration No:  ...                          Order No:      ...  ...  ...
                                               Customer No:  ...  ...  ...

Customer Address:                              Delivery Address:
Name   : .....................................................................
Street : .....................................................................
Town   : .....................................................................
PO Code: .....................................................................
County : .....................................................................
Note: This is a specimen
............ Despatch data.........................................
Delivery from    : ................... Your reference:......................
Terms of payment: .................... Account.....:......................
Currency         : .................... Price .......:......................
              <RETURN>=Continue    <F1>=Finish    <F2>=Stop
```

Fig. 3.1 — Example of a screen display.

(c) **Character-oriented interaction**: the computer acknowledges each input character.

Since screen-oriented interaction is the most common, we shall concentrate on this type. The response from the system is delayed until after it receives the transaction from the user. Therefore, the degree of interaction is relatively low and there are fewer immediate support and help facilities for the user. Although some of these limitations exist for technical reasons, we can achieve significant improvements by applying properly structured procedures and standards of software ergonomics.

3.3 PRINCIPLES OF VISUAL PERCEPTION IN THE DESIGN OF SCREENS

Information on a screen should be laid out in accordance with established principles of visual perception [1]. The laws of gestalt theory pyschology are particularly useful for designing screens.

The first law, the **tendency to organise**, states that, when a human being perceives groups or figures within his field of vision, he will structure what he sees according to clearly defined general properties such as simplicity and symmetry. Fig. 3.2 illustrates what is meant.

The second law, the **law of the good gestalt**, is made up of several factors:

(a) Similarity: elements which are the same or similar are drawn together into groups (e.g. with respect to colour or shape).
(b) Proximity: from otherwise similar elements, those elements are drawn together which are physically close to each other
(c) Symmetry: symmetrically arranged elements are drawn together

In order to display text on a screen so that it is perceived as a set of

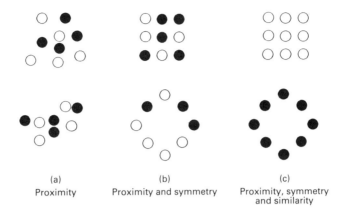

(a)   (b)   (c)

Proximity   Proximity and symmetry   Proximity, symmetry
and similarity

Fig. 3.2 — Illustrations of gestalt theory laws of visual perception.

homogeneous blocks, several factors in visual perception are usually at work at the same time. This is illustrated in Fig. 3.3.

There are two ways of reducing the visual and mental effort of the user. The first is to cut down the total volume of information on the screen. The second is to restructure the information by breaking it down into coherent units: this should enable the user to perceive and process the information more easily without reducing in any way what is actually displayed.

3.4 SOFTWARE ERGONOMIC TECHNIQUES FOR DESIGNING SCREEN DISPLAYS

Poor screen layouts are often the result of inadequate design procedures. Much better results could be obtained by breaking down the design process into three stages:

(a) the analysis phase
(b) content design
(c) visual design

Fig. 3.4 outlines what is required for each stage. The first job is to draw up requirements for the various tasks and user groups. We shall not consider this any further, as it is dealt with elsewhere in this book (see section 2.2.).

3.4.1 Task-related screen design
The first thing to consider is the contents of the data fields which the user will process on the screen. The separate data fields are usually hierarchically structured within a single record (e.g. for a customer order, first the customer's name, then the item ordered, delivery date, invoice details, etc.). The information needed for a particular transaction will not usually require all the information contained in a record. During the design phase it is essential, therefore, to decide how much redundancy should be built into

COHEN. G:
THE PSYCHOLOGY OF COGNITION;
ACADEMIC PRESS;
1983.

GREEN. T.R.G., PAYNE. S.J., VEER. G.C. v.d.
THE PSYCHOLOGY OF COMPUTER USE;
ACADEMIC PRESS;
1984.

HEILMANN. H:
HANDBUCH DER MODERNEN DATENVERARBEITUNG;
FORKEL-VERLAG;
1985.

Fig. 3.3 — Proximity and identity in displaying book references on a screen.

the screen display without reducing its overall clarity. There are two opposite approaches here. The first is to draw up tailor-made screens for each task. This produces a high level of redundancy in the system's data fields. The other approach is to preserve the content structure of the record, which increases the number of screen calls per task: the result is a higher transaction rate and takes more time. The two approaches must be weighed up against each other. The user will generally prefer to have more screens for tasks he does not carry out very often.

Large quantities of information can require the use of 'logical screens' in which the total amount of information is larger than a single physical screen display. This occurs where there are long lists of data items. The user can call up all the information by scroll or page functions (Fig. 3.5). Field scrolling is preferable for lists: information for the frame is retained on the screen while the user scrolls through the list entries.

Many systems have special information screens giving fast overviews of larger amounts of related data: other screens are available for the actual processing (i.e. inputting and altering data). The dialogue must ensure that the user does not lose track of where he is and what he is doing.

Finally, we consider possible conflicts of access authorisation.

Certain users might have to be denied access to particular screens or parts of screens. If so, we must take care not to destroy meaningful structure in a screen display.

A screen display contains various types of information which are necessary for interactive communication;

(a) information directly relevant to the task in hand, i.e. the data to be processed
(b) control information, i.e. the currently available functions
(c) status information, i.e. what is the current status of the hardware and software
(d) Explanatory information, i.e.
— error messages (e.g. input errors, exceeded time limits)
— help and instructions for the user (e.g. explanations of keywords, the next available processing operations)

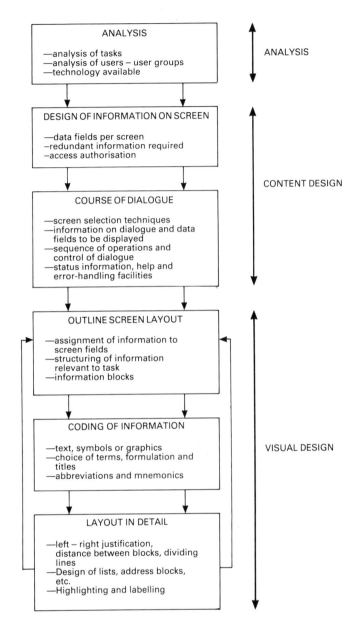

Fig. 3.4 — Stages in the design of screen displays.

3.4.2 Designing menus

Interactive screen dialogues can be controlled by different methods. These can depend, for instance, on whether the user accesses the system frequently or only on very rare occasions. Three common methods are

(a) selection of screens by transaction codes

Fig. 3.5 — Scrolling and paging.

(b) direct input of a command (e.g. the name of a data field)
(c) menus

Screens are often presented to the user in a set sequence which is determined by the program or the data items themselves: the user has little or no control. The system designer should at least ensure that the basic functions of jumping backwards, breaking off and interrupting the dialogue are available. In practice, fixed sequence dialogues are often unnecessarily rigid and could be designed to be much more flexible than they are at present.

Menus are a good example of user-controlled screen dialogues. Menus are hierarchically (tree-) structured levels of options by which the user calls up the various functions of the application software. The advantage is that the user sees clearly what functions are at his disposal, although it is not generally possible to manage entirely with a single menu level. Given several levels, however, the number of steps in the dialogue increases, which can be a hindrance to the experienced user. If possible, there should be no more than two levels.

How should we design the 'breadth' of a menu in relation to its 'depth'? Studies in West Germany [2] have shown that the time the user takes to choose an item from a list increases dramatically when the list has more than five to seven entries. This corresponds roughly to the short-term memory span for a human being. Longer menus should therefore be avoided. One way of doing this is to introduce a further menu level by creating new generic terms. If the terms in a list can be subdivided into two meaningful blocks, then the menu itself can be split into two separate menus side by side on the screen (Fig. 3.6).

For experienced users menus can be more of a hindrance than a help. There are ways of cutting down paths through menus. One method, for example, is to skip a submenu by inputting a special command. Another method is to set a line in the current dialogue to be the next screen to be processed.

The user may select a menu option by pressing a number key or a letter

Personnel dept. no.: 999999   MAIN MENU

Personal data   Salary

11 Private address   21 Income (commission)
12 Work address   22 Income (additional)
13 Dependents   23 Tax code
14 Age   24 Deductions (one-off)
15 Further details   25 Deductions (monthly regular)

                      00 Dialogue help

==> Selection : 99 Enter required number
                  (highlighted numbers only)

F2=Quit   F4=Screen 2

Fig. 3.6 — Example of a menu divided into two sections.

(preferrably the initial letter of the entry label): this is particularly suitable if the same keys can be used to jump directly from one screen to another. Otherwise, it is best to use the cursor. Other methods use a pointing device such as mouse and pop-up and pull-down menus.

3.4.3   The visual design of screens

3.4.3.1   General screen layout

A screen should contain information, not just on the task in hand, but also about how to control the dialogue and to handle the screen display. This particular type of information should be placed in fixed areas of the screen with its own action codes. There should be distinct areas on the screen for information related to the task, the dialogue, the status of the system, error messages and help facilities. Task-related information will take up most of the 24 lines on a standard screen and should be arranged so as to correspond to the usual sequence of processing operations, as shown in Fig. 3.7. If error

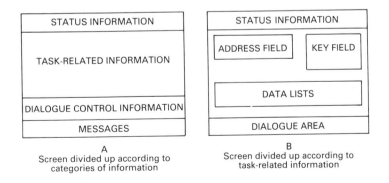

A
Screen divided up according to
categories of information

B
Screen divided up according to
task-related information

Fig. 3.7 — General layout of screens.

messages are displayed in the area of the screen where the mistake was made, they should be highlighted in some way. Task-related information falls into a number of typical and recurring categories:

(a) address blocks
(b) lists
(c) key fields
(d) plain text

The system designer can lay these groups out on the screen (or paper) before labelling them, etc. (see Fig. 3.7B). It is a great help to the user if the screen layout is standardised for a particular application, or even an entire data processing system.

3.4.3.2 Information codes

By information codes we mean the symbols (or series of symbols) which represent input and output on the screen. The symbols can be based on text, numbers, graphics or pictures. Even acoustic output is possible in certain cases. For character-oriented screens, only textual, numeric and semi-graphic symbols are possible.

Language-based codes

Successful communication relies on three things. The first is a shared vocabulary. The second is a knowledge of the concepts underlying that vocabulary and of the relationships between the concepts. The third is an awareness of the likely effect which information conveyed will have on the recipient (in our case, the user). This applies to communication in general as well as to user interfaces in data processing.

General-purpose applications intended for a wide circle of users will need to employ normal, everyday language. For highly specialised applications requiring knowledge of technical language, this will be possible only to a limited extent. In any case, data processing jargon should be avoided.

The room available on VDU screens is often small in relation to the information presented, which needs to be compressed or abbreviated in some way. Although this means that we no longer use language in quite the normal way, all the information can be clearly shown. Thus, a sentence such as 'Please enter the bank postal code', for example, is replaced with 'Enter post code' (the simple verb + noun construction is quite acceptable as a meaningful short form for a longer sentence).

If a term, such as the name of a data field, is made up to two or more words, then we should be careful about the order of words and their relation to each other. The less redundant word, i.e. the word carrying the most information, should come first, e.g.

OLD STOCK   and not   STOCK OLD
NEW STOCK   STOCK NEW

Negative questions should be avoided, since the reply can be misleading, e.g.

DO YOU WANT ANOTHER SCREEN?   YES/NO

and not

DON'T YOU WANT ANOTHER SCREEN?   YES/NO

Abbreviations

In the interests of clarity and comprehensiveness, only well-established and necessary technical abbreviations should be used. To preserve consistency, abbreviations should be standardised throughout an organisation (they could be collected in a standard reference booklet, for example). In some systems, up to six different abbreviations for a single term have been observed!

Special care must be taken to ensure that abbreviations do not lose or obscure the meaning of the original terms. Established abbreviations used in the everyday language should be retained, even if the user may be unfamiliar with the original long form. Examples are No., NATO, EDP, etc. Non-standard abbreviations, such as ACO (for automatic correspondence) or MoP (method of payment), present more of a difficulty. While there are no absolute rules governing the formation of abbreviations, we would recommend the following guidelines.

(a) *Omit vowels.* Because vowels have a higher functional redundancy than consonants, they can be more safely left out than consonants. Examples are Expl = Example, Cpy = Copy, Chrctr = Character. This is a particularly good method if the user has to reconstruct the original term from its abbreviation.
(b) *Omit part of the word.* Examples are Prov = Provision, Alt = Alteration, Cop = Copy. Omission of part (i.e. the end) of the word is recommended if the user will have to recall the abbreviation for later use (e.g. to input as a command).
(c) *Compound words.* Each component is shortened, thus Datalt = Date alteration. If one or more components are abbreviated, then those should be the least important ones, BuildingSocNo. = Building Society Number.

Headings

A screen may contain various headings or title terms. They are often combined with graphics symbols and serve as coded aids for subcategorising information into different groups. Each information block on a screen display should have its own heading (see Fig. 3.4).

Input techniques

There are various ways of (a) marking the point on the screen at which the user enters his input and (b) indicating the maximum field length available for the input.

If possible, the screen should indicate whether numeric or alphanumeric input is required. We could, for instance, use the full stop (.) to mark where numeric input is expected and the underline character ( ) either for alphanumeric characters or for a mixture of both. If decimal numbers are expected, this should be clearly indicated. Input and output formats should correspond exactly.

Where input fields require a decision, the options should be clearly displayed, e.g.

Make change? (Y/N): _

It is often known which option the user is most likely to choose. If so, we should assume a default response and pre-insert it. A different choice will, of course, overwrite the default:

Make change? (Y/N): Y

For key fields, we must show what the individual keys mean:

Title form: . (1 = Mr, 2 = Mrs, 3 = Miss)

If there is not enough room on the screen for the explanatory information, a help facility should be available. This could take the form of a screen menu summoned by input of the '?' character. When the user selects from the menu, the help information is displayed in the relevant field.

There are various methods for changing the contents of data fields:

(a) deletion of existing entry followed by the new input: the entries cannot be compared, but this method saves space on the screen
(b) direct overwriting: again, the entries cannot be compared and the method saves space on the screen, but the user is more likely to make mistakes
(c) the new input is displayed alongside the old contents of the data field: this takes up a lot of space on the screen, but both entries can be easily compared
(d) field editing: the user must learn how to use an editor, but the method saves screen space.

The advantages of (a), (b) and (d) is that there is no need to have different screens for changing data and displaying help information. However, an UNDO function is essential (for detailed advice on information design see [3]).

3.4.3.3 Detailed screen layout

In this last stage of design, the order and presentation of the information blocks are finalised, together with headings, field titles and the data fields themselves. It may also be necessary to change some of the information codes to achieve the best possible physical arrangement on the screen.

Left and right justification

When the user is quickly scanning the contents of blocks of information, most of his attention is focused on the boundaries of each block. Depending on the direction of reading, the left-hand side of a block is the most important. For this reason, related blocks, including headings, should be justified to the left (*cf.* Fig. 3.8).

Current No.	Income type (000)	From (date) (DDMMYY)	To (date) (DDMMYY)	Interest rate (00.00)	Total (00000)
1	123	01.01.80	31.12.80	07.25	12345
2	123	01.01.80	31.12.80	07.25	12345
3	321	01.01.80	31.12.80	07.25	54321

Fig. 3.8 — List headings.

Highlighting and labelling

Highlighting and marking draw the user's attention to important pieces of information on the screen, visually separating these from less important items. Only when he has exhausted all other forms of screen layout should the designer decide (a) what information should be highlighted and (b) what means of highlighting to employ. Highlighting can be carried out in the following ways.

(a) *Different brightness levels.* In practice, two levels of brightness are used, i.e. normal and highlighted. The highlighted area should remain legible even when the monitor is badly adjusted, Highlighting is useful for error messages and information which is not permanently on the screen.

(b) *Inverse video.* The designer should be careful not to have too many different fields in inverse video distributed over the whole screen. This destroys the effect of highlighting. It is better to combine fields in inverse video into a single block.

(c) *Flashing.* Flashing can very easily irritate the user. Only small groups of characters should be displayed in this way, and the designer should avoid making several parts of the screen flash at once. For characters which are to be read, the flash frequency should be about 1 Hz.

(d) *Altering the character type.* Different types of character can draw the user's attention to particular items of information. Certain terms may, for instance, be highlighted by upper case lettering. Otherwise, text should appear in a mixture of upper and lower case. Another possibility is spacing out the text, although this should not be used for long terms and labels because it makes them difficult to read.

(e) *Quasi-graphic symbols.* Quasi-graphic symbols are those which appear in the normal ASCII character set and which are suitable as a means of highlighting, e.g.

** Text **

These should be used sparingly. Possible examples are options on screen menus and 'if – then' links between fields.

Colour highlighting

The use of colours for highlighting should not be overdone. We suggest the following guidelines

(a) Physical and conceptual aspects of presentation should always take precedence over the use of colour.
(b) Colours should be used to group information sharing a common feature and must not be strewn about the screen (i.e. the presentation should be colourful, not incongruously motley).
(c) The user should be able to read characters and text easily against a coloured background.

REFERENCES

[1] Lindsay, P. H. and Norman, D. A. (1977) *Human Information Processing*, Academic Press, New York.
[2] Bartels, M. (1982) Untersuchungen zur Darstellung von Menüs. University of Stuttgart.
[3] Smith, S. L. and Mosier, J. N. (1984) *Design Guidelines for User–System Interface Software*, The Mitre Corp., Bedford, Massachusets.

4

Practical experience in designing software ergonomic projects for large application systems

H. von Benda

4.1 INTRODUCTION

The first question is: what do we mean by a software ergonomic project? We have deliberately chosen this term to mean two different things:

(a) research projects specifically in software ergonomics
(b) projects which have made use of software ergonomic principles

We shall report on both types of project in this chapter. Although we concentrate on the IBM user world, we do not consider this to be a real limitation, since the main features are also typical for other mainframe systems.

4.2 THE WORKSTATION

We can distinguish three types of workstation:

(a) unintelligent terminals connected to a host computer and central data base
(b) local workstations for decentralised data collection only: these have no direct link to the host computer or to the centrally stored data
(c) workstations with local intelligence and data storage capacity: they are also linked to the host computer and central data base

Until recently, the majority of workstations belonged to group (a). Type (b) workstations were often associated with batch processing centres where data collected on punched cards were converted to diskette, cassette or magnetic tape. Type (c) workstations carry out some processing operations on the spot (e.g. data validity checks), but are also directly linked to the host computer and central data base. (a) and (b) are typical for the IBM user world.

A typical workstation user would work within a particular area of the company, such as personnel management, accounts or breakages department. He would carry out fairly routine processing of documents (mainly forms of one kind or another). In the course of his work he would produce new documents (or parts of documents) and alter existing items of data.

4.3   REPORT ON A RESEARCH AND DEVELOPMENT PROJECT IN SOFTWARE ERGONOMICS

The project presented below was carried out between 1982 and 1984 by Stollman & Co. Ltd. in conjunction with the Institute of Psychology of the Technical University of Munich. It was supported by the BMFT (Federal German Ministry for Research and Technology).

4.3.1   Aims of the project
The main aim of the project was to answer the following question: which is ergonomically more suitable for a screen workstation — a transaction-oriented dialogue or a field–character-oriented dialogue? We assume that the user will be carrying out the routine processing tasks as described above. Although the question is primarily one of software ergonomics, in the final analysis it has implications for how we design an entire hardware and software system. These issues will be discussed in detail below.

First of all, let us explain what we mean by the terms 'transaction-oriented' and 'field or character-oriented'. A **transaction-oriented** dialogue is conducted as follows.

(a) The computer sends a screen to the workstation.
(b) The user fills in the empty data fields.
(c) The user presses a key to send the completed screen to the computer.
(d) The computer processes the screen. The first step is to treat the input for mistakes. If input errors are detected, the screen is sent back to the user for correction. The errors can be highlighted and accompanied by a more detailed textual explanation (usually only the first error is explained in this way).
(e) The user corrects the screen and sends it back to the computer.
(f) This procedure is repeated until all the inputs are error free. The computer then processes the data.

In a transaction-oriented dialogue the user is often confronted with very unclear and confused screen displays into which too much information (often using obscure abbreviations) has been squeezed. The reason for this is that the system has been designed with the technical and economic objective of keeping down the transaction rate and hence the processing demands on the computer. Therefore, it is important to accomplish as much as possible in a single transaction.

A **field-** or **character-oriented** dialogue differs from a transaction-oriented dialogue in one key respect. All input checks are made immediately after the input is made. Error messages and help information for each field are displayed as required.

4.3.2 Results of questionnaires

During the first phase of the project, workstation users from different areas of work (insurance companies, banks and public services) were interviewed about their workload, work requirements and work satisfaction. At first, the responses were all positive. Only after the software developers conducting the survey put specific questions and suggested possible improvements did a different picture emerge. For example, users working with a transaction-oriented dialogue were asked whether an input error check or field help message could increase job satisfaction and reduce their workload. Most were surprised and had not imagined that such suggestions could be implemented in the first place. 'That can't be done' was the commonest reaction. Once this view was corrected, field- rather than transaction-oriented interaction was felt in many cases to be a marked improvement.

Because circumstances and conditions varied so much for each user, the results of the questionnaire were not felt to be reliable. Differences arose in the keyboard used, lighting conditions, and the fact that colleagues or superiors were either present or absent during the interview. Because we wanted our results to be empirically sound, we decided to set up a laboratory experiment.

4.3.3 Laboratory experiment

First of all, we selected a typical area of activity (i.e. personnel) and, helped by professionals in that field, worked out what the typical tasks for that area would be. The tasks were then computerised (i.e. converted to different versions of interactive programs) so that the performance of users carrying out those tasks could be studied under laboratory conditions. Written questionnaires and interviews provided the data for evaluation. We attached great importance to the fact that all the interactive software was run on the same computer system (MAJA) under identical physical conditions and over the same periods of time.

The following interactive program versions were used.

Version I

This was an implementation of the transaction-oriented dialogue described above.

Version II

This used the same screen displays as in version I, with the addition of direct checking of field input, error messages and help information available for each field. The user was led through the screen a field at a time.

Version III

This version was similar to version II. The difference was that the user, by pressing a function key, could select any data field from the current screen or even from a different screen altogether. Inputting the field name took the user straight to that field.

Version IV

In this version the user was not presented with complete, ready-made screens. Instead he chose each field in the order he wanted by inputting the field name. In this way he built up the screen dynamically according to his own requirements.

The experiments were conducted with 25 users from various local government personnel departments from the West German Federal State of Baden-Württemberg. The results were as follows.

(a) The transaction-oriented dialogue is not generally suited to the tasks of this type of user. His unit of activity is mainly the data field.
(b) A form of dialogue based on complete, ready-made screens is suitable if the task involves inputting new sets of data or if the screen helps the user to see logical relationships between items of information more clearly (e.g. to gain a better view of entire sets of data). A sequential, field by field pathway through the system is only suitable if whole series of new data items are being collected. Otherwise the user feels the work is harder and less satisfying, especially if he knows that it is technically possible for him to switch from one field to another (both in the current screen and to others).
(c) A common activity is to change a very small number of data entries. Full screens do not help much here. The user would prefer to have direct and flexible access to a particular field. At the same time he should always be able to display — at a moment's notice and with a single key stroke — the whole screen to which a particular field belongs, should he need to re-orient himself.

The participants in the experiment reacted very positively to being able to write their own error messages and help information. This facility was available in the experiment and participants also used it to add individual notes for particular data fields.

For all versions throughout the experiment, system response times for accessing data bases were held constant. This was done in order to simulate the delayed responses which are typical of transaction-oriented dialogues. A delay of approximately 5 s was chosen.

Although a screen message was output for the response delay in versions II, III and IV, users felt the waiting time to be a real nuisance. They reacted by continuing to ask the system to let them carry on with the task, even when things were being held up. Clearly, parallel processing is a must from the point of view of user friendliness.

4.4   THE IBM USER WORLD

Large organisations have traditionally used mainframe computers for data processing. IBM is unquestionably the market leader here and can be taken as representative of commercial data processing practice. Computer architecture and operating systems are still basically oriented towards batch processing, although teleprocessing monitors have made interactive communication possible and transaction-oriented dialogues, as we have described above, are now commonplace. On closer observation, however, we can see that transaction-oriented dialogues are actually a split batch processing activity, the sub-parts being the individual transactions.

From the history of these computers and their operating systems it is evident that software ergonomics has played no part in the development of prevailing forms of dialogue. The main concern here has been to adapt old software with as little disruption as possible.

The world of the IBM user is thus dominated by large software packages which have been around for a long time now. The users (from heads of data processing departments down to end users at the terminal) live in a world in which the most important thing is compatibility. They have little or no opportunity of benefitting from modern and user-friendly forms of dialogue.

Recognition of the need for ergonomic software is slow to develop. It is true that large manufacturers such as IBM or Siemens have made a start by setting up laboratories to study ergonomic issues and by marketing computer systems for local processing. Traditional large-scale users of data processing, however, such as government organisations, insurance companies and banks, are still tied to old concepts and remain largely unreceptive to the demands of software ergonomics.

4.5   PRACTICAL EXAMPLES FROM THE FIELD OF PUBLIC ADMINISTRATION

For more than 15 years now, data processing has been in use in public and governmental organisations. Here, too, working practices are still dominated by batch processing.

In the mid 1970s some municipal computer centres in West Germany decided to introduce VDU workstations and data base systems such as IBM's information management system (IMS). One such centre was the Local Government Computer Centre for Hellweg-Sauerland. Users were equipped with dumb terminals linked to a central computer by data transmission lines (either dedicated or switched). This meant that users were totally dependent on the availability of the host computer and the connection to it. This kind of set-up requires very extensive supervision of the network and, where possible, back-up systems. The user at the terminal works with a transaction-oriented form of dialogue and response times deteriorate at peak periods when the system is busy.

From 1976 in the West German state of Baden-Württemberg, it was proposed that computing facilities should be decentralised by the introduction of intelligent data-gathering systems. Only in very rare cases were data bases transferred to the local systems owing to problems of redundancy in data storage. Tasks were allocated between the computer centre and the local system so that the processing was carried out, as before, in batch by the central host computer. The local systems, however, were able to access the central data base via data transmission lines in order to look up information. They were also responsible for all data collection and for checking the validity of input to data fields (checks against the contents of the main data store were still performed centrally).

Accessing and collecting data are, however, two separate processes. Since the central data store is not updated until some time after the data have been gathered (e.g. during a batch processing period), the information is not necessarily up to date. Although the installation described above avoids the problems of widely varying response times and of non-ergonomic processing of transactions, the user is still unable to process data items directly.

For these reasons, there have been moves in certain application areas towards direct online processing. This means that the ergonomic benefits of local intelligence and data storage are once again being abandoned.

Solutions to these problems, which affect the working conditions of several thousand users, are urgently needed. In general terms, we require systems which, for large organisations such as insurance companies, banks and government offices, combine central data processing and storage with the ergonomic advantages of local intelligence.

4.6   PROPOSALS FOR ERGONOMIC SOFTWARE

First of all we must acknowledge the practical fact that traditional methods of software development preclude participation by the user, who is only involved in the initial design stage. It is the software designer who draws up the specifications for the program. By then it is no longer possible to test these against the wishes of the user, who may not even understand the language in which they have been framed. The software product is developed in a linear, top-down manner. If the user asks for changes to be made — which he can only do once the whole thing is finished — they are effectively prohibited by their cost.

Clearly there is a need for a new approach which allows the user to be permanently engaged at every stage in the development of the software. In particular he should be involved from the very start in the design and production of the dialogue interface. This is technically possible with local systems running modular, user-friendly software tools. The interfaces for the actual processing system must be clearly defined. The screen design work (e.g. the screen layout, the error messages and help texts, the format of the data fields) can all be handed over to the user.

We still lack guidelines and standards for software tools which are themselves ergonomic and which are capable of providing user-friendly interfaces. The paucity of empirical studies also means that we are unable even to draw up a checklist for ergonomic application software. Only when the results of such research become available will we have uniform standards for ergonomic dialogue interfaces.

Until that time comes, we must draw on what little we know about software ergonomics and develop the best systems we can by involving the user as much as possible.

We shall now briefly describe a system for a workstation which is almost fully implemented.

In the system, work is allocated between the mainframe and a local intelligent workstation. The mainframe carries out the main processing tasks and serves as the central data store. The local system controls the entire dialogue and handles data input. It has its own data description library (data dictionary), rules for performing validity checks and pre-processing programs. The user at his local workstation constructs and manages his own error messages and help information, which are stored on his machine. He can also design or change his screen displays without affecting the interface to the mainframe processor. Fig. 4.1 shows the applications involved.

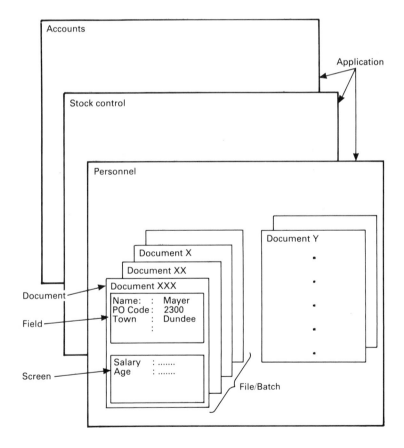

Fig. 4.1 — Examples of data processing applications.

The functions of the user's machine are broken down into different levels which we shall refer to as **abstract machines**. The levels are shown in Fig. 4.2.

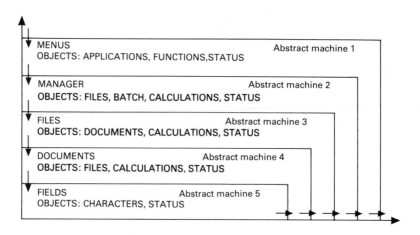

Fig. 4.2 — Local intelligent workstation with its various functional levels.

The different levels, or abstract machines, are defined by their objects and the operations performed on those objects. Each level can be developed and tested on its own. Furthermore, the software can be designed and produced top down and bottom up by programmers and users working in close cooperation.

We are convinced that such systems are a way forward for the future. They offer the best prospect of significantly improving the ergonomics of on-line processing without the need to re-write the entire software.

5

Knowledge-based human–computer interfaces and software ergonomics

R. Gunzenhäuser and Th. Knopik

5.1 INTRODUCTION

It is true that software technology has made great strides in developing effective tools for science, engineering and other specialised fields. However, a lot of work still needs to be done to integrate these tools into application-oriented systems with good interfaces for dialogue-based communication. For example, many application packages are supported by isolated and unique dialogue systems. The applications themselves have been developed independently of the actual dialogue interfaces (this is true of systems for airline ticket booking, travel and timetable information, invoice production, software for planning journeys, etc.).

For local workstations, however, dialogue interfaces are being increasingly used in conjunction with applications of this kind. For example, the user might fill in information from application forms into data fields on screen, and then use a text processing system to write the necessary correspondence, and finally produce the figures and accounts from a spreadsheet program.

In the future, we will see these integrated applications used more and more in distributed systems. One user at an intelligent workstation will be able to plan all aspects of a journey, ranging from booking accommodation and arranging the means of transport to attending to the personal requirements of the traveller. The actual reservations will be made via computers on local or wide area networks. When the journey is over, data are entered for the invoice, verified by receipts, and passed on to the central accounts department.

5.2 THE USER AGENT

In a system such as the one we have just described, a single user could run from his workstation any number of different application programs, either on his own computer or on others linked up to his network.

Ideally there should be a separate functional level or interface between the user and his 'tools' (by which we mean any kind of application software, from a text processing system to a programming environment). The purpose of this interface is to attend to all the interactions between the user and the computer, taking full account of (a) the particular features of the task and the processing software and (b) the general and individual requirements of the user himself.

We can call this interface a **user agent**. Such a user agent would take the form of a fully integrated and portable unit and would incorporate every-thing needed for an effective interface between the user and the software which he is running.

In order to implement a generalised user interface of this kind, we need to develop techniques for describing methods of communication which are specific to humans and computer systems (so-called **dialogue models**). As a starting point we shall refer to known forms of interaction:

(a) formal command and query languages
(b) menus and windows, also in conjunction with icons and pointers
(c) graphics manipulation
(d) (limited) natural language

Since the aim of dialogue modelling is to design powerful and effective dialogues, we also need to take account of research in the following areas:

(a) models of communicative behaviour relevant to information processing
(b) interdisciplinary studies in informatics and linguistics
(c) formal descriptive methods for drawing up specifications for dialogues
      (e.g. transition diagrams)

It is also important to know how to introduce into human–computer interaction the kind of knowledge which people conducting a dialogue have about each other and which plays an important role in successful communi-cation. In real-life dialogues the participants use such knowledge to form mutual conceptual models of one another. Similarly, in computer-assisted dialogues, the computer also has to acquire and store knowledge about the user. Such a **knowledge-based user model**, to which the user agent has access, would provide a sound basis for on-screen help facilities and instructions.

In traditional models of dialogue the user communicates with his application program (e.g. an editor or a graphics display package) directly via an interface which is unique to that program. This has a number of drawbacks.

(a) A separate interface must be designed and implemented for each application program. This increases development costs.
(b) The specifications for this interface become complicated because the semantics of the command language are often mixed up with those of the operations and objects of the application program.
(c) Non-standard user interfaces are likely to emerge because of the different conventions adopted by various applications.

(d) Integrating different software tools can at best only be accomplished
with *ad hoc* solutions.

In a generalised user interface, communication should only take place
via the user agent. This makes the interface, which converts the user's
instructions and queries into program-specific commands, independent of
the particular software tool or application (*cf.* Fig. 5.1).

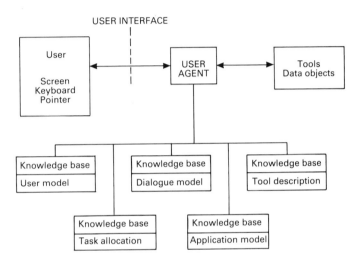

Fig. 5.1 — The user agent.

While the human user is communicating with the system, the user agent
is supported by various knowledge bases. These are as follows.

(a) The **tool description**. This contains information about the objects being
manipulated by the tool or application program. These could be texts
and the operations which the program can perform on them, such as
formatting.
(b) The **dialogue model**. This informs the user agent about the history of the
dialogue so far, general strategies for communication, possible forms of
interaction, and specific transformations either from the command
language into an internal intermediate language or from the output of
the application program into a particular form for the user. The user
agent is able to switch from one form of interaction to another at the
appropriate point.
(c) The **user model**. This contains information about the user which is
relevant to the communication. It includes his intentions (insofar as
these have been abstracted from the dialogue so far), his assumptions

and strategies, cognitive abilities, limitations, motivation and understanding of the system.

(d) An **application model**. This represents the relationships between the
different applications and their approaches. It allows the user agent to
select the correct software tool. It also integrates the activities of various
tools in carrying out a particular task.

(e) **Task allocation**. This coordinates the activities of members of a team
who may be working at different locations on a project.

Research on individual knowledge bases has reached different stages.
Progress in formal methods for tool descriptions, for example, is more
advanced than current work on user models.

5.3 THE CONSTRUCTION OF KNOWLEDGE-BASED SYSTEMS

Over the last few years designing knowledge-based systems has become an
important research discipline in its own right. The results are already in
commercial use in so-called expert systems. We can look at these from the
following points of view.

(a) *The representation of knowledge*. The aim here is to arrive at a
formalism for representing conceptual structures, inference rules and
heuristic rules which is independent of a particular subject area.

(b) *Programming languages for representing inference processes*. These
are tools which allow programs to be written on the basis of a formalised
representation of knowledge. These tools include higher level programming languages which have emerged from research into artificial intelligence (AI). Examples are PROLOG and frame-structure oriented
languages such as ObjTalk, which has been developed by G. Fischer, J.
Laubsch and C. Rathke at the Institute for Informatics at the University
of Stuttgart [1].

ObjTalk is an extension of LISP. It combines a frame-structured
knowledge representation with the object-oriented approach, in which
data and procedures are encapsulated in 'active' objects which communicate with each other by means of 'messages'. One of ObjTalk's
current applications enables a user to enter newspaper reports into a
knowledge base [2].

ObjTalk is also being used and extended at Stuttgart in INFORM,
which is part of the WISDOM group project supported by the Federal
German Ministry of Research and Technology (BMFT). This project is
looking at techniques for the visual presentation of information and for
screen-oriented communication in an office environment [3].

(c) *The construction and management of knowledge bases*. Special systems
allow the subject specialist to build a knowledge base for his own
application model or software tool. He requires no expert programming
knowledge.

(d) *Kowledge bases in distributed systems*. In networked computer systems we need to be able to classify the objects in the various knowledge bases so that we can assess the requirement for each data base.

In Europe and the USA various models and languages are currently being developed for knowledge bases (especially expert systems). Examples are:

(a) production systems such as OPS5 (Official Production System Version 5 is a rule-based programming language for producing expert systems in industrial applications) [4]
(b) object-oriented approaches such as UNITS [5]
(c) logic programming using PROLOG

Two projects, RITA [6] and COUSIN [7], are directed at using such systems for generalised user interfaces. Both employ production systems as the control structure. In COUSIN the tool description is based on an object-oriented representation. The work of Moran [8] is especially relevant for the design of the dialogues.

5.4 TWO EXAMPLES OF DIALOGUES

At this point we will give two examples to illustrate the fact that traditional dialogue strategies are inadequate for user interfaces designed to react flexibly to users' requirements. Such systems require knowledge in order to 'understand' the inputs of the user and respond with appropriate answers.

Example 2a (Fig. 5.2a) shows how, in traditional computer-assisted

C: What is $2 + 2$?

U: *Four*

    COMMENTARY: The user could also have input 4, IV, 16/4, or 4.00. Even in such a simple situation as this it is not easy to predict the total set of all possible right answers. In this case, whoever set up the dialogue had not thought of "four" as a correct answer. The computer therefore responds as follows:

C: Wrong. Would you like help?
    Answer with "yes" or "no".

    COMMENTARY: 'Wrong' is not an appropriate response to the user's input. The user recognises that the machine has not understood and tries another 'correct' answer, disregarding what the computer is currently asking him to do.

U: *4*

C: I do not understand "4"!

    COMMENTARY: The computer tests the answer to its last question and cannot assign it to either "yes" or "no". It returns to where it was before it has asked the user whether he wanted help. The user, on the other hand, is getting frustrated and expresses his feelings as follows:

U: *If you don't understand 4 either, how are you supposed to teach me mathematics?*

    COMMENTARY: For this input the computer carries out a keyword analysis, finds '4' and responds with:

C: Correct. Very good!

Fig. 5.2a — An instructional dialogue without a knowledge base.

instruction, a dialogue might be conducted in a system without a knowledge base. The dialogue is between a user U and a computer C. We attach a commentary to each interaction.

The well-known ELIZA program written by Weizenbaum [9] uses a similar dialogue interface to that shown in example 2a. It, too, is based on analysis of keywords and makes little use of semantics to recognise relationships between items. Systems of this kind create in the minds of users the impression that they 'understand' natural languages and can solve problems with intrinsic knowledge. That, however, is the very thing they do not do.

Example 2b (Fig. 5.2b) is an example of a dialogue from Bobrow's genial

C: Hello, my name is GUS. I can help you plan a simple trip by air.
    Where do you want to go

U: *I want to go to San Diego on May 28*
    COMMENTARY: By providing more information than GUS asked for, the user is taking over the conduct of the dialogue. This shows that fixed inbuilt dialogue sequences cannot be used for this type of application.

C: What time do you want to go?

U: *I must be in San Diego before 10 a.m.*
    COMMENTARY: The user's answer is only indirectly related to the question.

C: Would you like PSA Flight 102 that arrives at 9:15 a.m.?
    COMMENTARY: The system tries to accommodate the user. As the user did not specify the departure time (only the time of arrival), GUS answers accordingly.

U: *What is the next flight?*
    COMMENTARY: Here, too, the initiative changes. By this direct question the user takes over the conduct of the dialogue.

C: Air California Flight 310 that leaves at 8:30 a.m. and arrives at 10:00 a.m.

U: *I will take the first one*
    COMMENTARY: GUS must decide what 'the first one' refers to from the context.

C: In what name shall I make the reservation?

U: *Technical Academy, Esslingen*

C: I have confirmed the following: PSA flight 102 on Wednesday, May 28, from San Jose to San Diego that leaves at 7:30 a.m. and arrives at 9.15.
    COMMENTARY: To confirm the result of the dialogue, GUS summarises once again all the information about the reservation.

Fig. 5.2b — Dialogue between a customer and an airline booking system with a knowledge base.

understander system (GUS) [10]. It simulates the role of an airline employee who is conducting a conversation with a customer. In the sample given here, the customer wishes to purchase a simple return ticket to a town in California.

By drawing on its knowledge base, GUS displays the cooperativeness which one would expect in an 'intelligent' dialogue system. This is because GUS allows the initiative in the conversation to switch from the computer to the user and back again. It is also able to process indirect questions, to handle backward references to items mentioned previously, and to 'understand' incomplete sentences as answers, supporting its own interpretation with known conversation patterns.

The example clearly demonstrates how a knowledge base and inference rules can be used to make dialogues between human users and computers more truly interactive and 'intelligent'.

5.5 USER MODELS AND HELP FACILITIES

Adequate help systems and tutorial programs are vital for all types of human–computer interaction. While tutorial programs give initial training in operating the hardware and the application software, help systems provide on-line support to the user at his workstation (e.g. in the form of context-dependent help messages, screen displays of reference manuals, keyword-oriented help texts, or special explanatory dialogues). If help facilities can be personalised, then so much the better. To implement these we need a suitable model of the user. This consists of a knowledge base containing information about the user or user groups.

In developing user models, studies have been undertaken in several areas:

(a) The underlying cognitive capacities of the human being (e.g. visual perception, memory, structures of representation, models of language) have been examined.
(b) Ergonomic analyses to establish the demands which different types of work place on the user have been carried out.
(c) Types of user have been examined. This is to establish and analyse relevant characteristics of various categories of user. Analysis is based on education, vocational training, frequency of interaction with the computer, and any other factors which may affect performance.
(d) User acceptance and motivation have been studied.

Since about 1974, prototype user models for dialogue systems have been under development at several research centres in the USA. A highly significant result of this work is that, if a dialogue system is to provide active help for the user, it must possess knowledge about his aims and assumptions, his familiarity with the system and also his cognitive abilities. In actively helping the user, the system takes the initiative and intervenes in the dialogue to output an error message, an item of information or a warning. This contrasts with passive help facilities, in which the user — perhaps after making a mistake — asks the system for assistance.

In Fig. 5.3 we introduce and explain the distinction between **static** and **dynamic** help. Active and passive help systems can provide both static and dynamic help facilities.

In the Stuttgart research project, INFORM, two different help systems have been developed, i.e. an active and a passive one [11].

The passive help system is implemented in OPS5 for a text editor. The

PASSIVE help requires an explicit request for help	ACTIVE help is given if the system establishes that the user has made a mistake
STATIC help provides information about fixed structures in the program	DYNAMIC help takes into account the specific environment in which the request for help is made

Fig. 5.3 — Help systems.

user inputs help requests in restricted natural language form (e.g. 'How do I get to the beginning of the next line?'). A problem-solving module then generates the appropriate help message on the basis of the analysed input and the current state of the editor. When providing help, the system explains to the user one step at a time and in natural language what he has to do ('Put the cursor on the desired line'), which editing command to use ('Give the instruction for "cursor down"') and what keys he must press ('Press the DOWN key'). Only when the user has done this correctly does the system output the information for the next steps ('Now go to the beginning of the line', 'Give the instruction for "set to beginning of line"' , 'Press the keys: CRTL-A').

The active help system is implemented in ObjTalk and Franzlisp for a text editor which monitors the user while he is at work. It automatically gives him help and directions if his performance is below a certain level. This occurs under two conditions. The first is where the user, instead of inputting a single complex command, employs a series of simpler commands. The second arises if the user does not activate a known command with the minimal number of key strokes. The system is equipped with 20 different 'plans' for recognising at any one time what the user is doing or trying to do. One such plan, for instance, is 'erase the part of the word to the left of the cursor'. If the user does this by repeatedly pressing the delete key, then the plan picks up the fact that more key strokes have been used than necessary. It then works out what help to provide by looking at the status of the editor and consulting a simple model of the user: it will also check what ready-made help strategies are available. For this particular case it would draw the user's attention to the 'rub out word left' command which is activated by pressing the 'ESCAPE-H' keys.

In providing help the system constantly refers to its model of the user. This contains a statistical record of how often the user, for a particular operation or plan as described above, has done the following:

(a) carried out the operation
(b) carried out the operation as efficiently as possible
(c) used wrong commands
(d) used too many key strokes
(e) received a help message

The help strategy is flexible and determined by several factors:

(a) the minimal period of time which should elapse between one help message and the next
(b) how often the user is allowed to carry out the operation inefficiently before he is given help
(c) the maximum number of help messages which should be output for any one operation
(d) the number of times the user performs a particular operation perfectly before it is no longer monitored.

Even expert systems are usually equipped with help facilities. The main problem here is the extent to which the user participates in the system's internal inference or deduction processes. In cases of doubt the user might want the system to explain to him the reasons for suggested courses of action which it has output to him. The reader is referred here to the work of (a) the Stanford Research Institute (SRI) on task-oriented dialogues, (b) Carnegie--Mellon University of 'graceful interaction' and (c) the University of Pennsylvania on user participation in interactive problem solving.

The need to incorporate help facilities into dialogue systems for software tools was recognised at an early stage. This led to the development of explicit techniques for representing knowledge, such as semantic nets.

Help for the user can be provided in tutorial form, i.e. as a computer-controlled question and answer dialogue. It can also allow for 'controlled navigation' through a knowledge base. The main thing is that these help systems are dependent on a model of the user. Rich [12] describes a system for user modelling which controls the help which is output on the basis of explicit information provided by the user himself and general knowledge about groups of user characteristics (so-called stereotypes).

If we consider how our model of a 'user agent' could provide help facilities for particular software applications, we can say that it would take account of the following factors:

(a) the expectations of the user about how the application works, i.e the operations it performs and what the output signifies
(b) the user's objectives, strategies and assumptions
(c) the cognitive abilities of a user, e.g. demands on short-term memory and attention

Everything in the user model either (a) is already available in an explicit form or can be elicited (providing user profiles), or (b) emerges implicitly from the dialogue and its context. The system needs implicit knowledge to decide, for example, whether an instruction by the user corresponds to his actual intentions. In the event of a discrepancy, the system can initiate so-called explanatory dialogues. If we are to achieve more of a symbiotic (i.e. truly cooperative) relationship between the user and the software tool, then our dialogue interface will have to take account of such implicit objectives and intentions.

5.6 THE COMPLEXITY OF USER MODELS AND HELP STRATEGIES

Producing suitable user models is a complex business, even for quite simple dialogues. Very simple techniques are still being used in traditional computer-assisted learning. For example, the program may count up the number of correct, incorrect and 'unexpected' answers input by the user. Average response times and other straightforward items may also be recorded. The information is constantly updated while the user is running the program and may be accessed from a data file, either for testing the learner or even monitoring the questions themselves.

Much better user models may be found in educational games. Wumpus is a well-known example. By wandering around in a network of about 25 nodes, called caves, the hunter must discover the whereabouts of a monster, the Wumpus, and kill it with an arrow. The Wumpus lives at a randomly selected node. Moving through the caves the hunter encounters various dangers.

(a) Many caves have pits into which the hunter may plunge to his death.
(b) Many caves have bats which may drag the hunter into another, randomly chosen cave.
(c) If the hunter shoots into a cave which does not contain the Wumpus, the arrow may rebound off the walls and kill him.

The computer creates the network of caves and distributes the dangers at random.

The educational value of the game is derived from the fact that the player (the hunter) learns how to assess the impending dangers before every move. He does this by weighing up different probability values for each danger, which issues a clear 'warning'.

(a) The bats squeak, which can be heard in the adjacent caves.
(b) The pits emit a draught, which can be felt in adjacent caves.
(c) The smell of the Wumpus can be detected up to two caves away.

Given these warnings and what he already knows about the cave system, the player can work out the best moves for the hunter. To win, the player must kill the Wumpus with one of his small stock of three arrows.

There are several implementations of this game. Each uses a wide range of different rules or a least varies the number of caves, bats, pits and arrows.

The computer shows the hunter–player a section of the cave network, his current location and the dangers which are detectable from his position. By inputting a number of a cave, the player chooses the next cave he wants to enter. This is a simple choice from the menu of available caves. Other input displays directions about which caves he may or may not enter and the rules of the game. Almost every inplementation includes a help command for calling up this information.

As a rule, a high resolution graphics screen is needed to display the cave network, unless only a very small portion of it is to be shown. A list of the caves which the player has entered so far and of the dangers he has detected can also be output. Although provided as an additional facility, the list representation is essential for small screen monitors. Figures 5.4 and 5.5 compare the two types of display.

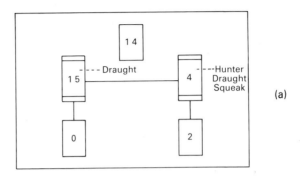

(a)

CAVE	ADJACENT CAVE	WARNINGS
15	0 14 4	Draught
4	14 15 2	Draught Squeak

(b)

Caves	/0 1 /2 3 /4 5 6 7 8 9
	10 11 12 13 14 15
Pits	
Bats	2
Hunter	15

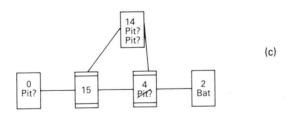

(c)

Fig. 5.4a — Graphic display.
Fig. 5.4b — List.
Fig. 5.4c — Combined graphic display and list.

Studies have been made as to which of the displays players prefer. Displays with no graphics at all were widely rejected. Most positively assessed was the combination of screen graphics and list, an example of

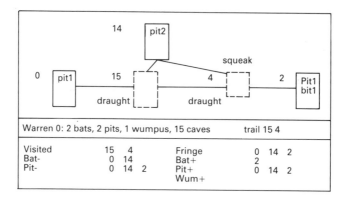

Fig. 5.5 — Screen display of game.

which is shown in Fig. 5.5. Here the anticipated dangers (pit and bat) are included in the graphics display as well as in the straight list. Under pit+ and bat+ are listed those caves which are known to contain no hazards of this kind.

As the game involves a learning process, it must be adaptable to different groups of users. Firstly, the game provides for different levels of play.

(a) A version for beginners with a small cave network, few dangers and detailed help facilities.
(b) A version for more experienced but nevertheless weak players. This has a complete cave network and a lot of dangers, but also detailed help facilities. One of our implementations provided a 'guardian angel' to warn the hunter of dangers and to prevent him from making a fatal move.
(c) A version for very good players with no help facilities.
(d) A version in which two hunters (at separate screens) compete with each other.
(e) A version which is adapted to specialised forms of dialogue, such as teletext screen displays.
(f) A version for blind players.

This adaptability is based on different models of the user and different help facilities.

The version shown in Fig. 5.5 uses a relatively sophisticated model of the user. It registers exactly which rules or levels of play have been understood by the user and which have not been so far.

The WUSOR II version by Goldstein [13] envisaged the player progressing through five successive phases of learning. While the game itself manages with about 25 rules of probability and strategy, the player acquires a knowledge of the following in gradual stages:

(a) rules for different states of play
(b) rules for distinguishing different states of play
(c) rules for evaluating states of play
(d) rules for assessing probabilities
(e) rules for working out the numerical probability of the next best move

The user model also monitors the order of precedence in which the learner acquires these rules.

WUSOR III goes one stage further. The rules of play are represented by inference rules which are used to work out the optimal move for each particular state of the game. The rules are embedded into a so-called 'genetic graph' as nodes, where the adjoining edges represent the relations between the rules. Examples of relations are

(a) analogies between rules
(b) generalisations about rules
(c) refinements or simplifications of rules

In models such as this, rules can be combined into groups to which certain general laws apply. The user model notes which groups each player masters and which he does not.

In user models such as the one we have just described, knowledge about the players is accumulated during the game and deposited in a knowledge base. This knowledge base may contain ordered sets of data in the form of semantic networks or frames (in the sense of Minsky). Because such knowledge representations are derived from research into artificial intelligence, learning strategies of this type are often referred to as 'intelligent'.

5.7   THE USER AGENT AS TUTOR

Until now considerable experience from computer-assisted learning has gone into developing 'intelligent' user interfaces (as in WUSOR). In educational systems a so-called **tutor** often takes the role of user agent. The tutor has the following important features.

(a) A series of (tutorial) strategies are available on request.
(b) A stock of explanations and help messages can be called up directly by the user.
(c) Algorithms which decide which directions, explanations and help messages to give for a particular situation are used. The decision will also depend on the best way to proceed and on what is contained in the user model.

Such algorithms are not easy to construct because there is no uniform procedure for deciding when the tutor should intervene in the interaction. Should it, for instance, give help whenever a mistake is made, or should it allow the user to make non-critical errors and perform at a level which is less than efficient? As yet, this is an area about which we know very little.

Similarly, there are only a few systems which are able to make reliable deductions about the causes of wrong responses by the user. Models capable of doing this have until now only been developed for simple learning situations, such as learning how to perform arithmetical operations with numbers [14].

An important feature of a tutor is the way in which information is output to the user. The design, form and layout of the output can be related to specific groups of learners or to particular tasks. It is also affected by special knowledge about the communication and its form which has been gathered during the dialogue itself.

Fig. 5.6 indicates how an 'intelligent' tutor can be supported by a series of

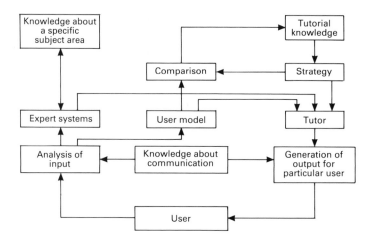

Fig. 5.6 — The 'intelligent' tutor.

knowledge bases. In this model the tutor has access to knowledge in the following areas:

(a) the field of expertise (facts and methods)
(b) the learning strategies
(c) procedures for diagnosing errors
(d) the form of communication (e.g. natural language input and output)
(e) the user
(f) help facilities

Although there is currently no known system which combines all these components, it is clear from Fig. 5.6 that such a model could be regarded as a prototype for a general-purpose 'intelligent' interface for application systems.

5.8 SUMMARY

Human–computer interfaces still exhibit major deficiencies from the point of view of software ergonomics. The main reasons for these deficiencies are as follows.

(a) Many application systems are unique and exist in isolation.
(b) Interfaces do not conform to a common standard. They are also inflexible and cannot be adapted to the needs of the user.
(c) There is insufficient support for the user, both during the introduction of a system and its day-to-day operation.

These deficiencies could be overcome if interfaces were standardised during the development stage and employed expert systems approaches. It would also help to apply the experiences of computer-assisted learning. The objectives should be:

(a) to integrate application systems at the workstation and to network them with other workstations
(b) to maintain a standard interface for all applications
(c) to design the interface in such a way that it can be externally adapted to the needs of the user, or even adapt itself
(d) to give the user full computerised support facilities when he starts to use the system and to continue to do so for as long as he wants it

These are essential objectives if we are to see any improvement in the software ergonomics of computer systems.

REFERENCES

[1] Rathke, C. and Laubsch, J. (1982) *Report of the German Chapter of the ACM*.
[2] Hanakata, K. (1980) An intelligent digester for interactive text processing. *Proc. COLING-80, Tokyo*.
[3] *Wisdom* 84 (1984) Application to the BMFT.
[4] Brownston, L., Farrell, R., Kant, E. and Martin, N. (1985) *Programming Expert Systems in OPS5*, Addison-Wesley, Reading, Massachusetts.
[5] Smith, R. G. and Friedland, P. (1980) A users' guide to the UNITS system. *Technical Report*, Heuristic Programming Project, Stanford University.
[6] Anderson, R. H. and Gillogly, J. J. (1976) Rand Intelligent Terminal Agent (RITA): design philosophy. *Report R-1809-ARPA*, Rand Corporation, Santa Monica, California.

[7]   Ball, E. and Hayes, P. (1980) Representation of task specific know-
      ledge in a graceful interacting user interface. *Report CMU-CS-8-123*,
      Department of Computing Science, Carnegie–Mellon University.
[8]   Moran, T. P. (1981) The command language grammar: a represen-
      tation of the user interface of interactive computer systems. *Int. J.
      Man–Machine Studies* **15** 3–50.
[9]   Weizenbaum, J. (1967) Contextual understanding by computers.
      ACM **10** 474–480.
[10] Bobrow, D. G., Kaplan, R. M., Kay, M., Norman, D. A., Thomson,
      H. and Winograd, T. (1977) GUS, a frame-driven dialog system.
      Artificial Intelligence **8** 155–173.
[11] Fischer, G., Lemke, A. and Schwab, T. (1985) Knowledge-based help
      systems. *CHI '85, Human Factors in Computing Systems, San Fran-
      cisco, April 1985.*
[12] Rich, E. (1979) Building and exploiting user models. *Report CMU-CS-
      79-119*, Carnegie–Mellon University, Pittsburgh.
[13] Goldstein, I. (1980) Developing a computational representation for
      problem-solving skills. In: D. T. Tuma and F. Reif (eds.) *Problem
      Solving and Education: Issues in Teaching and Research*, Lawrence
      Erlbaum Associates, Hillsdale, New Jersey.
[14] Brown, J. S. and Burton, R. R. (1978) Diagnostic models for proce-
      dural bugs in basic mathematical skills. *Cognitive Sci.* **2** 155–192.

6

Knowledge-based systems and communication between computers and human beings

G. Fischer and M. Herczeg

6.1 INTRODUCTION

When computer systems are being developed, attention is often focused on problems of technical detail. It is important, however, not to lose sight of the following objectives.

(a) Computers should relieve human beings of as much work as possible. This is especially true for work which is beyond our ordinary mental capacity. It also applies to tedious routine tasks and to work of a dangerous nature.
(b) Computers should be made accessible to more people. Users should not need a training period of several years in order to utilise a computer system effectively.

These objectives depend not so much on producing fundamentally new hardware, better operating systems and programming languages (where progress is easier to achieve), but on the results of research into knowledge-based systems (KBS) and human–computer interaction (HCI). For this we need to develop suitable tools and to test these in prototype applications.

6.2 DESIRABLE FEATURES OF FUTURE COMPUTER SYSTEMS

6.2.1 Human-oriented systems

Scientific and technical progress in the last 20 years has produced steady advances in the ability of computers to communicate with their users. First of all compilers made it possible to write programs in high level languages — one of the first moves towards relieving humans of the need to adapt themselves to the computer instead of the other way round. High level languages marked a shift in emphasis from 'how' to 'what': in other words, instead of the user having to tell the computer how to resolve a problem in the form of explicit, step-by-step instructions, he can present the problem itself, leaving the computer to use its knowledge to find a solution.

If we accept the need for human-oriented systems, then we must reverse the traditional direction of systems development. Instead of computer systems being developed from the 'inside outwards' (i.e. given the hardware, software is designed for it and, finally, a user interface is added on), they need to evolve from the 'outside inwards'. This means defining the technical and social environment in which the computer will be used before creating the right kind of software and hardware.

In the past, technology has evolved principally in order to support human motor and sensory functions (examples are the hammer and the microscope). The particular challenge to information technology lies in extending human cognitive abilities. In other words, the computer should reinforce human intelligence.

6.2.2 Symbiotic systems

Symbiotic systems are based on enhancing human skills using the computer as an aid to perform a task which neither man nor the computer can carry out alone. In many areas problems have become so complex that humans can no longer manage without computer support.

Studies (for example, on pilots and employees in nuclear power plants) have shown that people perform significantly less efficiently if forced to adopt a passive role. Working constantly below the level of their capabilities prevents them paying full attention to the task and, if necessary, actively intervening in it.

There is an essential distinction between symbiotic systems and those in which the human being plays a minor, monitoring role. In the latter, we are dealing with automatic, self-regulating processes in which he has to content himself with the mental equivalent of working on a conveyer belt. A key feature of symbiotic systems is that both partners need to communicate in order to carry out a task together. In such systems we see tasks being allocated between the user and the computer as follows:

The human being
    (a) provides the objectives
    (b) provides comprehensive general knowledge
    (c) splits a problem up into constituent parts (subtasks), defines them and specifies their relationships to each other
    (d) builds on previous experiences
    (e) integrates knowledge from various fields
    (f) solves problems by using analogies to draw conclusions
    (g) chooses suitable representations and displays
    (h) monitors the solutions to the subtasks.

The computer
    (a) acts as an external aid to memory (to store large amounts of information and intermediate results)

(b) provides levels of abstraction (because procedures, packages and modules can be defined)

(c) controls the effects of changes and tries to avoid or uncover inconsistencies

(d) clearly presents the consequences of our assumptions (by allowing us to use Popper's method of critical error removal [1])

(e) breaks up complex information structures and conceals irrelevant details

(f) directs our attention to important results (e.g. by visual means such as colour, inverse video, flashing)

(g) allows the consequences of actions to be reversed (UNDO command), promoting investigativeness and creativity.

6.2.3 Convivial systems

The notion of the **convivial tool** was coined by Ivan Illich, which he defines as follows [2].

'Tools are intrinsic to social relationships. An individual relates himself in action to his society through the use of tools which he actively masters, or by which he is passively acted upon. To the degree that he masters his tools, he can invest the world with his meaning; to the degree that he is mastered by his tools, the shape of the tool determines his own self-image. Convivial tools are those which give each person who uses them the greatest opportunity to enrich the environment with the fruits of his or her vision. Tools foster conviviality to the extent to which they can be easily used, by anybody, as often or as seldom as desired, for the accomplishment of a purpose chosen by the user.'

One of Illich's main concerns is that the individual is being increasingly deprived of the consciousness of being able to shape his environment actively. This fear of being controlled is surely one of the most important motivations for the current hostility towards technology and computers. Illich argues for taking science out of the hands of a clique: science should strive to simplify tools so that everyone can have the opportunity of shaping his immediate environment.

Tools are convivial if people can master them in their lives and work, understand them and learn how to use them — in other words, if the tools can be thoroughly penetrated by human thought and action. One of the main dangers for human beings is that they adapt themselves to tools without fully understanding them, accumulating a mass of knowledge about limited applications and only partially comprehending the elements which they manipulate.

The statement 'software is not soft' sums up the current situation in the use of computers. From the point of view of the user, we can define hardware and software as follows:

(a) **Software**: all parts of a computer system on which the user can exert a formative influence

(b) **Hardware**: all parts, which, once present, can no longer be modified.

If we accept these definitions, then current computer systems appear to the user to consist almost entirely of hardware. The main concern of our research is to increase the proportion of genuine software in computer systems and to enable the user to alter and adapt a system to suit his own requirements.

In contrast to most other information technologies, such as television, teletext and videodiscs, which are passive (i.e. the user is not generally able to influence their design and basic function), the computer allows the user to assume an active, formative role. The ability to be modified by the end user is of fundamental importance in open-ended systems (such as an office), since it has now become impossible to foresee all possible requirements (i.e. actions and circumstances) which may arise at any one time. This means that traditional data processing systems, which carry out or provide support for precisely specified tasks, will have only a minor role in the future.

At this point we should clear up the following possible misunderstandings before they arise.

(a) The user should not necessarily be required to master future systems of this kind overnight. Expert use of such tools presupposes careful and long-term effort (even to drive a car one needs a driving licence).
(b) KBS have developed in such a way that the human user has surrendered more and more control to the computer (i.e. the 'what' has replaced the 'how'). At first sight this looks like an anticonvivial tendency. However, users were not particularly concerned about having this control in the first place — just as many drivers are happier with an automatic gearbox. Computer users had no desire to control the machine directly (for example, to give it memory storage addresses), preferring to exploit it as an intelligent tool for carrying out their tasks.

6.2.4 Ergonomic systems

Approaches adopted in traditional ergonomics are not adequate for problems which arise in information technology. Modern computer systems should support the human user in solving problems, making decisions, planning and other cognitive activities. Software ergonomics, therefore, must look at a whole variety of issues. These range from the design, analysis and evaluation of computer software to human perception, thinking and actions, as well as the actual content of the work itself, the processes involved and the environment in which it is performed.

Our objectives and experiences in the field of software ergonomics can be summarised in the following set of propositions.

(a) *The limited resource in information processing is human attentiveness and not the information available.*
Modern techniques of communication have meant that the volume of information has been steadily increasing. Almost every person nowadays has access to more information (e.g. in books, films) than he can

possibly process in his entire lifetime. The really limiting factors are the time and the attention which a human has at his disposal to process such large quantities of information [3]. One of the most important things a computer must do, therefore, is to make information available, to summarise it for the user, and to present it in a sensible form.

(b) *Computer systems designers must take into account different types of human memory.*
One of the most important factors in human cognitive behaviour is the limitation imposed by short-term memory. 'Recognition memory' and 'recall memory' are two types of memory which access information in different ways. In menu selection systems, for instance, only recognition memory is used. Systems requiring inputs in a command language, however, make demands on recall memory.

(c) *Systems designers should exploit the ability of human beings to process visual information efficiently.*
Techniques of visual presentation (graphics, colour, windows, etc.) open up new possibilities in this area.

(d) *The user should be able to construct for himself an adequate model of the system's functionality (how it works and what it is supposed to do).*
To the extent that the user is only interested in a particular application, he need have no knowledge of the deeper levels of the system (e.g. operating system, programming language, file system).

(e) *Computer systems should be adaptable to different types of user.*
This means that computers should either adapt automatically to the needs of different users (i.e. they are **self-adaptive**), or the end user should be able to adapt the system himself (i.e. they are **adaptable**). There is no such person as 'the' user of a computer. Every user has a different level of familiarity with the system as well as expertise in his own field. He has a certain aptitude in assimilating visual information and in operating a keyboard or pointer. Personal characteristics of this sort are not immutable and the systems designer cannot provide for them as though they were. Systems which are self-adaptive or adaptable should offer the user ample opportunities for shaping the user interface.

(f) *Different application systems being run by a single user should have a standard user interface.*
Standardisation of user interfaces is essential if computer systems are to be used efficiently and if there is to be a free transfer of know-how about how to perform different tasks. For example, the frequent user of a screen editor does not need to think consciously about the actions required to move the cursor about the screen (an analogy is clutch control on a car). If he changes over to another application, the same actions are carried over either consciously or subconciously. If the user is to perform a task with maximum efficiency, we must avoid making him frequently switch backwards and forwards between different conventions.

(g) *User interfaces must be developed by experts and conform to specified requirements.*

The need for proper expertise and clear specifications in designing user interfaces is equal to that demanded of application specialists and programmers in producing application systems. The user interface has a decisive effect on the quality of work which can be achieved with the system. It should also be standardised for different applications. This means reversing the traditional process of system development: instead of developing systems from the inside outwards, the opposite direction should be taken, so that the application is embedded into the interface and not the other way round.

(h) *The user should be able to reverse (UNDO) operations carried out by the system.*

Many activities (such as design, planning, construction) require the user to explore a wide range of potential solutions to a problem. If a result is unsatisfactory, he should be able to return to a previous state by means of UNDO functions.

6.2.5   Intelligent systems

The main aim of research into KBS and human–computer communication should be to transform the computer from a mysterious, incomprehensible and inaccessible machine into a useful and reliable tool which can make life easier. Computer systems must contain information about themselves which can be presented to the human user and explain its own actions to him in a form which he can understand.

We cannot accept a situation where computers provide information and data for important decisions while at the same time they do not permit the user to see how such information has been arrived at. KBS are complex because they are models of complex relationships in the real world. This means that systems need both to conceal complexity from the user and also to allow him to make the computer 'justify' its output.

How intelligent should systems of the future be? If considerable efforts are not made to make the new technology accessible to a large section of the population, then what scientists think of as progress will, in ordinary people, produce feelings of alienation and subordination to power. Whether we use computers as genuine aids or are controlled or even dominated by them will depend, not so much on the nature of computers themselves, but on the way we use them.

We cannot as yet be certain of the possible limitations of computer applications. Nonetheless, we may assume that the changes which will result from the wide-ranging use of computers will be as far reaching as those of the industrial revolution. We shall have to come to grips with the following developments.

(a) *Changes in the labour market resulting from office automation.*

The restructuring of the labour market should not be carried out without due regard to social consequences. We must not overlook the fact that research workers concerned with how computers can be used as tools to make life easier will not be the ones to play a major role in their actual introduction. The decisive impulse here will come from a largely profit-oriented section of society.

(b) *The computer as an instrument of control.*
This issue centres on rules of data protection. The critical aspect here is, not what is technically possible, but the aims and intentions of computer users.

(c) *Changes in work.*
How can we prevent human beings from becoming cogs in what are mainly automatic systems and how can we stop people's working lives being dominated by dull, routine tasks? The WISDOM project at the University of Stuttgart aims to create computer systems which are oriented to human beings, and not computer-oriented humans [4].

6.3 KNOWLEDGE-BASED SYSTEMS AND HUMAN–COMPUTER INTERACTION

KBS and HCI are interdisciplinary technologies and are important for a large number of different developments in the field of information techno-logy. Research in HCI cannot be restricted exclusively to forms of communi-cation (e.g. dialogues in natural language or speech as opposed to formal languages) or to the visual presentation of information on the screen. If the system has no knowledge base, communication can only be very limited. Our research is based on the established fact that communication and knowledge are inseparable (see Fig. 6.1).

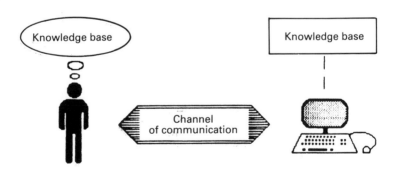

Fig. 6.1 — Model of KBS and its user interface.

A human being possesses, not just expert knowledge of his own particu-lar subject area, but also knowledge about how to solve problems, methods of communication and his dialogue partner. This kind of knowledge is as important for an interactive computer system as for human beings.

Fig. 6.2 shows a traditional system in which communication is highly restricted because the knowledge base is very small.

In ordinary human communication, a good analogy to HCI without a knowledge base is a situation where someone can talk well but, at the end of the day, does not have much to say (Fig. 6.3). An example of this is the STAR system by XEROX: although it has a nice user interface, it is inadequate for certain tasks which require a degree of internal knowledge.

Extensive knowledge without the ability to communicate (Fig. 6.4) is equivalent to somebody knowing a great deal but not being able to pass this knowledge on to others. Examples of this are found in expert systems developed in Stanford with which the user can only communicate via a teletype-oriented interface.

Our aim should not be to present the entire contents of the knowledge base at any one time, because it is the attentiveness of the human being and not the information itself which is limited. By introducing intermediary filters (Fig. 6.5) the information can be presented in a way which suits both the user and the task in hand.

An evaluation of the Dipmeter Project revealed that the outlay for development was as follows [5]:

Inference	8%
Knowledge base	22%
Feature recognition	13%
User interface	42%
Production environment	15%

This example clearly shows the high outlay involved in equipping an expert system with a good user interface. Indeed the actual inference component required the least effort.

There are three central problem areas in implementing KBS.

(a) *Acquiring the knowledge.*
Knowledge must first of all be 'fed' into the system. This knowledge exists initially in the minds of human beings and it is frequently a laborious process getting it from there and into the machine. Often, the individual finds it difficult or even impossible to formulate his knowledge in an explicit form.

(b) *Representing the knowledge.*
A number of mechanisms for representing knowledge have been developed in recent years. Our own, ObjTalk, is an object-oriented language in which knowledge is represented by classes and instances embedded in a hereditary network (see Chapter 5, section 5.3).

(c) *Using the knowledge.*
A system with a large knowledge base is not much use if it cannot make

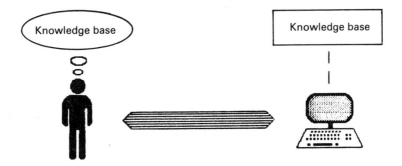

Fig. 6.2 — Traditional system.

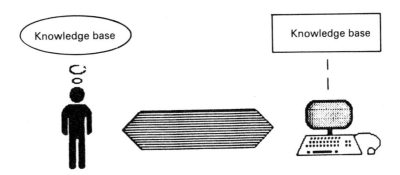

Fig. 6.3 — Good HCI without an extensive knowledge base.

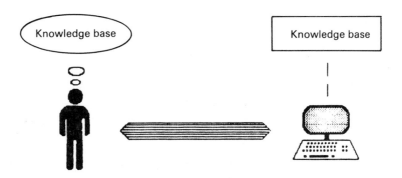

Fig. 6.4 — Knowledge base with poor HCI.

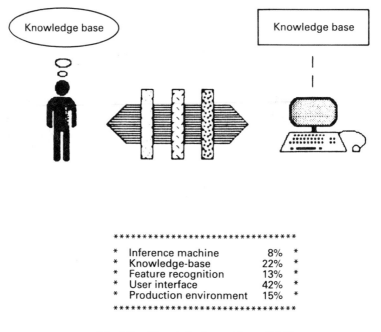

```
********************************
*   Inference machine       8%  *
*   Knowledge-base         22%  *
*   Feature recognition    13%  *
*   User interface         42%  *
*   Production environment 15%  *
********************************
```

Fig. 6.5 — Knowledge base with good HCI.

the knowledge available in an appropriate manner and at the right time. The contents and precise structure of a large knowledge base are not generally known to the new or occasional user. He needs to be familiar with the names and structures of the data objects to find and manipulate them successfully.

6.4 EXAMPLES OF KNOWLEDGE-BASED SYSTEMS WITH GOOD USER INTERFACES

In this section we present outlines of two prototype systems which have been developed in the INFORM research project.

6.4.1 FINANCE: knowledge-based form processing

FINANCE is a system for office use. It supports the processing of forms containing dependency structures (see Fig. 6.6) and can be regarded as a knowledge-based extension of Visicalc.

The system is used for producing financial plans for project applications. The following features are implemented:

(a) construction of a knowledge base with ObjTalk: the dependency structures are implemented with the aid of so-called 'constraints'
(b) information presented in windows: the size and contents of each window can be changed with icons and pointers

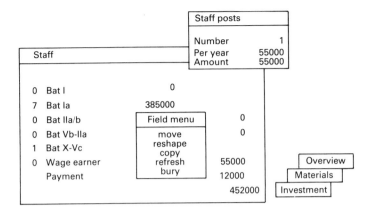

Fig. 6.6 — FINANCE: knowledge-based form processing.

(c) menus and icons
(d) filters to represent (internally stored) information in different ways for different purposes
(e) fully integrated help facilities.

These features can be used for a wide spectrum of similar tasks, such as filling out a tax form or a travel expenses claim.

6.4.2   PLANNER: computer-assisted planning

PLANNER is used by students of information processing in planning the second part of their course. We can regard the program as consisting of two parts:

(a) an **expert system** which is a kind of student academic counsellor
(b) a **personal assistant** which helps the user in complex planning problems.

The system was implemented on a colour graphics terminal, so that Fig. 6.7 can only give an inadequate picture of the system and its capabilities. PLANNER uses the applications-independent user interface developed for the DYNAFORM system [6].

Among other things, the knowledge base (which was also implemented with ObjTalk) is used for the following.

(a) To make suggestions to the user (on the basis of limitations which he has communicated to the system).
(b) To help the user to resolve conflicts in his course planning.
(c) To generate multiple perspectives with filters defined by the user himself. For instance, a large amount of information is associated with a particular lecture course (optional or compulsory, name of lecturer, where held, time, content, etc.), and only some of it will be relevant to the user.

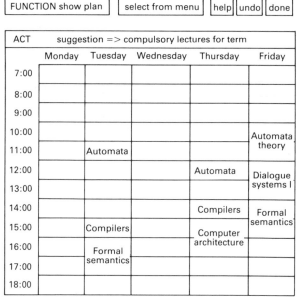

Fig. 6.7 — PLANNER: computer-assisted planning.

(d) To relate local and global planning strategies to each other. Local strategies affect planning for a particular academic session. Global strategies are concerned with the longer term implications of decisions.

(e) To present information of a more individual or personal nature. The system builds up a model or profile of the user over a long period. This model can be examined and modified by the user at any time. Its function is similar to the picture which a real academic counsellor would build up of a student after a series of face-to-face consultations.

6.5 FOCAL POINTS FOR FUTURE RESEARCH

Although some of the problems involved in making computers more 'intelligent' either have been solved or at least are now more clearly understood, we are still only at the beginning of the road. The following issues still require urgent attention.

(a) Technology by itself is not enough. We need to learn more about how human beings communicate and how to represent information (e.g. in office applications).

(b) We must develop new techniques of interaction. These will be less oriented to properties of hardware and outdated programming methods and more towards natural methods of communication as used by human beings.

(c) User interfaces must be adaptable to as many different types of user as possible.

(d) Studies have shown that the capabilities of information systems are not being fully exploited: the degree of utilisation is often less than 50%. Improvements in HCI are urgently needed to raise this level of effective use.

(e) For help and tutorial systems [7], it is not enough merely to devise a software solution to a particular problem: the solution must also take account of how the user himself works and behaves.

(f) User interfaces must be designed as powerful and applications-independent environments for as many systems as possible.

(g) Many different kinds of knowledge have to be represented in computer systems. Further methods of acquiring, representing and using knowledge must be developed.

(h) We also need representations of 'meta-knowledge'. This will allow us not only to add new information to a system in a way which is simple and consistent but also to explain and restructure existing knowledge. KBS should also know what they do not know.

(i) Current systems can only solve problems which are relatively clearly defined. If we are to make further progress (e.g. in computerising the office), we will need to develop open-ended systems which the end user himself will be able to modify.

(j) Systems should also be able to integrate their activities and decisions into larger contexts than at present.

REFERENCES

[1] Popper, K. R. (1959) *The Logic of Scientific Discovery*, Hutchinson, New York.

[2] Illich, I. (1973) *Tools for Conviviality*, Harper and Row, New York.

[3] Simon, H. A. (1981) *The Sciences of the Artificial*, MIT Press, Cambridge, Massachusetts.

[4] Bauer, J., Böcker, H.-D., Fabian, F., Fischer, G., Gunzenhäuser, R., Herczeg, M., Maier, D., Rathke, C., Riekert, W.-F. and Schneider, M. (1984) *Report of the INFORM Research Group*, Institute for Informatics, University of Stuttgart.

[5] Smith, R. G. and Baker, J. D. (1983) The Dipmeter Advisor System. A case study in commercial expert system development. In: *Proceedings of the Eighth International Joint Conference on Artificial Intelligence, IJCAI-83, Karlsruhe*, pp. 122–129.

[6] Herczeg, M. (1983) *Report to the German Chapter of the ACM*, Stuttgart, pp. 135–146.

[7] Fischer, G., Lemke, A. and Schwab, T. (1985) Knowledge-based help systems. In: Borman, L. and Curtis, B. (eds.) *Human Factors in Computing Systems, CHI-85 Conference Proceedings, New York*, pp. 161–167.

7

Input–output devices for human–computer interaction

H. Balzert

The user interacts with the computer by means of input–output devices. The technical evolution of these devices has been the main factor in setting the limitations for human–computer interaction and in deciding what freedom the software ergonomist has in designing suitable interfaces. The aim of this chapter is to outline current and future I/O devices for human–computer interaction and to assess the effects on the design of ergonomic software.

Historically, human–computer interaction began with punched cards for data input and printouts of the processed output. The first major step forward was made when teleprinters were linked to the computer. Rather as with the ordinary typewriter, the user would input data a line at a time and he would receive printed output the same way: the orientation to lines was necessitated by the technology of the teleprinter itself.

Video display terminals and screen workstations opened up new possibilities for handling input and output. Screen monitors — instead of continuous paper in a teleprinter — provided a two-dimensional display area for new forms of dialogue based on screen menus, windows, etc. Screens with 24 to 25 lines and with 80 characters per line are now standard and the keyboard user can position the cursor anywhere on the screen. As a result, the standard I/O device for human–computer interaction is now a character display screen equipped with a keyboard incorporating cursor keys and additional function keys.

Using cursor keys (the cursor can generally only move a single character or line at a time) proved to be very time consuming, especially when graphics screens and 'windows' came on the scene. Because graphics screens, unlike character display screens, do not have a large visual unit like a character, fast and precise positioning with cursor keys is not possible. As alternatives, the following pointing devices were developed:

—mouse
—joystick
—tracker ball
—light pen

—graphics tablet
—touch-sensitive surfaces

7.1   THE MOUSE

A mouse [1–3] is a small, neat box with one, two or three switches on the top
and a roller ball on the bottom (see Fig. 7.1). The mouse is placed on a

Fig. 7.1 — Different types of mice.

smooth surface, where it can be moved to and fro with ease. The movement
of the mouse is imitated by a cursor on the screen, allowing the user to select
characters, words, instructions or pictures, etc. Actions can also be initiated
with the switches.

Apart from the mouse with a roller ball (mechanical mouse), a variation
is available which has no mechanical parts and is sensitive to a patterned
surface (optical mouse). While the mechanical mouse works on almost any
table surface, the optical mouse needs a special underlay with a patterned
grid.

The resolution of a mouse is about 200 points per inch (approximately
one point per millimetre). Typically, 1 in of movement by the mouse
corresponds to 2.5 in on the screen.

Advantages
(a) Given the switches on the mouse, the keyboard is only needed to
     input text. Almost everything else can be done with the mouse.

   (b) The mouse rests beside the screen on the table or desk-top and the user has it immediately to hand.

   (c) The mouse can be adjusted to different degrees of sensitivity, i.e. the movement of the mouse does not have to correspond 1:1 to that of the cursor.

   (d) Users quickly get used to handling the mouse.

   (e) The load on the user's cognitive abilities is minimal. The error rate is low and the mouse can be positioned quickly.

Disadvantages

   (a) Space on the desk-top must be kept free for the mouse and its movements.

   (b) It is another item of equipment on the desk-top.

   (c) It cannot be used to input graphics or handwritten text.

   (d) It is not suitable for portable computers.

   (e) The mechanism is often unreliable (the roller ball gets dirty).

   (f) It is difficult to position correctly for small points on the screen.

7.2   THE JOYSTICK

A joystick [4] (Fig. 7.2) is a device for pointing. It consists of a control stick

Fig. 7.2 — Joystick.

or arm which can be moved by the user in at least four directions. Control signals are transmitted to the computer corresponding to the stick's direction of movement.

We can distinguish between **digital joysticks,** in which the computer understands only the direction of movement, and **analogue joysticks,** which transmit the strength of a change in movement as well as the direction itself. Analogue joysticks, for example, can be used with linear potentiometers and can be switched either to return automatically to the central position or to free float, i.e. the stick remains in the position it was last left in. Joysticks are especially popular for video games.

Advantage
    (a) It needs less space than the mouse.

Disadvantages
    (a) It has a higher error rate than the mouse and takes longer to position.
    (b) It is unsuitable for inputting graphics and text.

7.3 THE TRACKER BALL

A tracker ball (Fig. 7.3) is a freely revolving ball which can be moved with

Fig. 7.3 — Tracker ball.

the fingertips. This movement is converted into a corresponding cursor movement on the screen.

    The tracker ball is essentially an upside-down mechanical mouse. It has the same advantages and disadvantages as the joystick.

7.4 THE LIGHT PEN

The user communicates with the computer by pointing the light pen (Fig. 7.4) at an actively illuminated screen (cathode ray tube) [5].

Fig. 7.4 — Light pen.

A light pen can be used in the following ways.

(a) Images (e.g. options in a menu list) are displayed on the screen. The user points to an image to activate the computer.
(b) The user points to the screen to generate output at that position. The output could be a dot or graphic character for free-hand drawing.

Light pens have been used for some time in computer-assisted design (CAD). A light pen is constructed with a light-sensitive tip (photosensor) which detects the light emitted by the screen. The position on the screen is determined by comparing the timing of the light emissions.

Advantages
(a) The user can point directly to an image.
(b) Graphics input is possible.

Disadvantages
(a) The user must sit close to the screen.
(b) The user must pick up the light pen every time he wants to use it.

This means that he often has to take his eyes away from the screen to look for it.

(c) Light pens often have no switches, so they can only be used in conjunction with a keyboard.

(d) Light pens cannot be used with passively illuminated screens (e.g. liquid crystal displays).

(e) Frequent use tires out the arm muscles.

7.5   THE GRAPHICS TABLET

A graphics tablet (Figs 7.5a and 7.5b) [6–8] is a rectangular board which

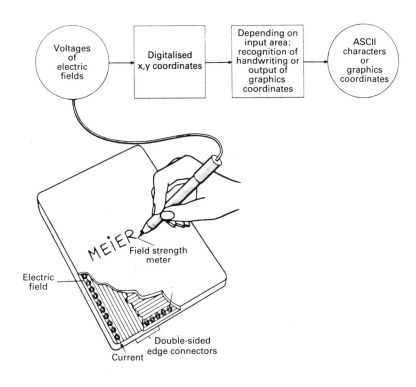

Fig. 7.5a — A graphics tablet.

accepts input from a pen or a movable magnifying lens with crosswires. Its mode of construction varies with the application and the resolution required. One method is based on the principle of magnetic coupling. Here, the tablet contains a grid of wires in which a moving magnetic field is maintained. A coil in the pen picks up the field signal and sends it to a phase comparator circuit. Depending on the method used, resolution can be between 0.5 and 0.0025 mm.

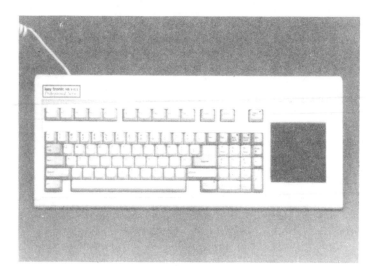

Fig. 7.5b — Keyboard with integrated graphics tablet.

Advantages
(a) It is highly suitable for graphics and text input.
(b) Absolute positioning is possible since every point on the screen is assigned a unique point on the active surface of the tablet (exact imaging).
(c) Touching the surface of the tablet positions the cursor instantly to the corresponding point on the screen, regardless of where it was before.
(d) Paper overlays can be placed on the tablet and traced over.

Disadvantages
(a) If a pen is used, it must be picked up every time it is needed (see light pen).
(b) The pen often has no switch (unlike the versions with magnifying lens and crosswires). If so, it can only be used together with a keyboard (see light pen).
(c) The tablet must always be present as an underlay.

In some applications users find the presence of a tablet irritating.

An **acoustic digitiser** (Fig. 7.6) functions without a tablet. An ultrasonic transmitter in the pen emits a signal when the user presses the pen onto a surface such as a desk-top. Two microphones fixed at opposite points detect the signal and calculate the position of the pen (to an accuaracy of 0.1 mm). The sonic transmitter can be switched to constant transmission mode, in which 100 signals are emitted each second.

Triumph Adler has incorporated an acoustic digitiser in its own experimental model of a manager's workstation (see Fig. 7.7). Here a flat plasma

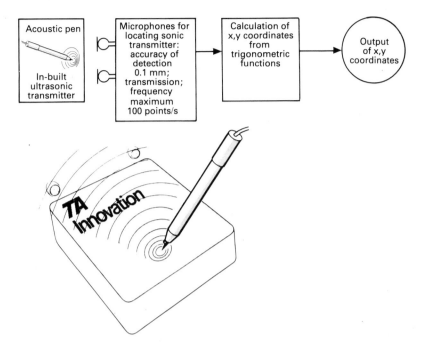

Fig. 7.6 — An acoustic digitiser.

Fig. 7.7 — Photograph of an experimental model of a manager's workstation made by Triumph Adler.

screen is built horizontally into the desk surface. With an acoustic pen the user can now point directly to menus, windows and images on the screen. In constant transmission mode handwriting or graphics can be drawn on the screen, where it appears immediately (unlike a ballpoint, the pen itself does not write as such [9]).

7.6 TOUCH-SENSITIVE SURFACES

Touch-sensitive foil surfaces (Figs 7.8 and 7.9) [10–12] respond to the pressure of a finger or any kind of pen.

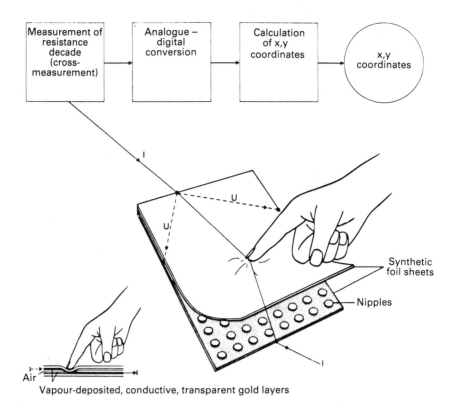

Fig. 7.8 — Touch-sensitive, transparent foil sheet.

Different types of touch-sensitive surface are available, depending on the application.

(a) *Mechanical*

Two transparent synthetic foil surfaces, incorporating vapour-deposited gold particles and separated from each other by studs or nipples, are pressed together, allowing an electric current to pass at the point of

Fig. 7.9 — Screen with infrared transmitters and receivers.

pressure. The position of the current is determined by cross-measurement.

(b) *Infrared*

Infrared transmitters and receivers are located at opposite edges of the screen. If any object interrupts the paths of the infrared beams between transmitter and receiver, it produces a signal which pinpoints the position at which the interruption occurs.

(c) *Capacitive*

A glass plate is covered with a thin metal layer which almost conducts electricity. If the plate is touched, such as with a finger or a metallic object, an electronic circuit recognises the capacitance difference between the point touched and the surrounding area: this indicates the position of the point.

The first technique has been used by Triumph Adler in two applications.

In the first application, the manager's workstation, a foil sheet is placed over the flat plasma screen set into the desk-top. With a QWERTY board overlay, the user can input characters by touching the keys as shown.

In the second application the foil sheets are attached to the left and right hand sides of the keyboard. When the user moves his finger across the sheet, the screen cursor traces the action (i.e. the sheet functions as a 'static mouse': see Fig. 7.10).

Many manufacturers also use these foil sheets on cathode ray tube screens, allowing the user to point directly at the screen. From the user's point of view, the method is similar to that of the light pen and has the same disadvantages.

Advantages
    (a) The user can point directly at the object, either with a pen or finger.
    (b) Any kind of pen can be used and it has no cable to the computer.
    (c) If menus are used, no keyboard is needed.

Disadvantages
    (a) Fingermarks make the screen dirty.
    (b) The user may have to sit close to the screen.
    (c) Frequent use is a strain on the arm muscles.
(d) The angle at which the user must sit in front of the screen can present visual and ergonomic problems.

7.7   COMPARISON OF POINTING DEVICES

Card *et al.* have compared the mouse, joystick, cursor keys and function keys in terms of their efficiency and ease of use [13]. The aim of the study was to find out which device is best suited as a pointer for text processing in terms of pointing, error rate and the size of the object being pointed to. Of the four devices, the mouse emerged as without doubt the best for selecting text on the screen (see Fig. 7.11).

At this stage we can only speculate about the future development of sensor devices which will be able to react to voice, eye movements or even thoughts [14].

A device is already on the market which uses light-emitting diode technology (similar to remote television controls) to move the screen cursor. Called NOD, it requires the user to carry a plate the size of a small coin. The NOD itself is a little box on the screen which picks up the movements of the plate by the light reflections and converts these into cursor movements [15].

In general, we should note that getting users to accept new technology is always very difficult where it increases their dependence on equipment.

7.8   ICONS AND POINTERS

The combination of pointers, graphics screens and pictures opens the door to a new form of dialogue in which the user directly manipulates the objects on the screen. In some respects this is similar to the physical office environment, where objects (e.g. forms or documents) are visually identified, picked up and processed [16] (see Fig. 7.12).

7.9   HANDWRITTEN INPUT

In the future we shall see an increasing need to input information in handwritten form (Table 7.1). Handwriting is, after all, the most wide-

Fig. 7.10 — Using touch-sensitive foils as a 'static mouse'.

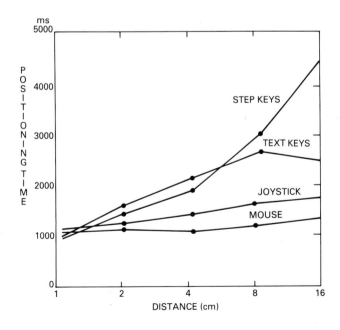

Fig. 7.11 — Positioning time in relation to distance from object [13].

Fig. 7.12 — System M32: an example of a desk-top computer in which the user
directly manipulates the objects on the screen.

spread technique of producing text. For managers in an office it is normal
practice to add comments to existing documents or to make notes in
longhand.

Two types of handwritten input can be distinguished:

(a) handwritten input without text recognition
(b) handwritten input with text recognition

In the first case the computer records the text as a bit pattern. This is
adequate for many applications where the only requirement is that the input
can be read again on a graphic screen, either by the person who input it in the
first place, or by others.

In the second case the handwriting is recognised and processed by special
software and converted to ASCII characters. Current systems are able to
recognise handwritten capital lettering to a satisfactory standard of speed

Table 7.1 — Techniques for the input and recognition of handwritting

Technique	Application	Current techniques	Future techniques
Handwriting			
Recognition of handwriting	—Mail distribution —Keywords for information retrieval	Recognition of printed writing; slow handwriting; normal speed not recognised; any size; commercially available	Recognition of fast hand printing at normal speed.
Handwritten input	—Handwritten notes and memos —Comments and corrections to documents —Signatures	Input via acoustic digitiser, graphics tablet; display on graphic screen.	Input via normal writing pens.

and reliability (see the section on graphics tablets for an outline of the technology involved).

7.10 SPEECH RECOGNITION

There are three qualitative levels of speech recognition:

(a) word-by-word speech recognition (see Fig. 7.13)
(b) recognition of word chains
(c) recognition of continuous speech

Word-by-word speech recognition means that the computer is able to recognise individual words with sufficient pauses between them. In (b) it recognises sentences broken up into word chains and in (c) those spoken normally.

For all three levels we can distinguish between **speaker-dependent** and **speaker-independent** recognition. Speaker dependent means that a particular speaker makes the required vocabulary known to the system by repeating it several times. The computer extracts from this the individual speech characteristics of the speaker and retains them as a reference model for recognising future speech input. For speaker-independent recognition the computer does not need such a 'learning' phase. The simplest system is word-by-word speaker-dependent speech recognition. The most complex is a continuous, speaker-independent model (see Table 7.2).

Studies by Triumph Adler's Basic Research and Development Division into experimental models of workstations for managers and secretaries (see Figs 7.14 and 7.15) have given the following results (each workstation is equipped with a 200 word speaker-dependent speech recognition system).

(a) Speech input is highly popular with users, who frequently use it as an

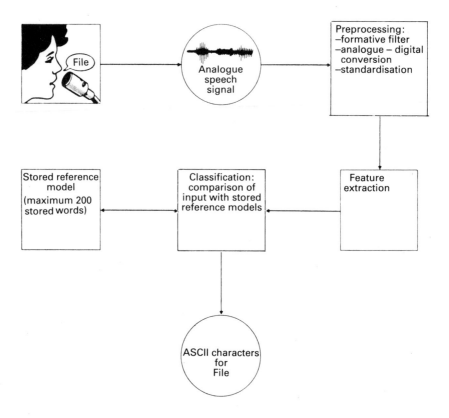

Fig. 7.13 — The principle of word-by-word speech recognition.

additional, optional method for calling up application software and performing operations of a very general nature.

(b) The speech recognition rate is extremely high. Once the computer has learned the vocabulary (each word is spoken three times), the rate remained unchanged after six months.

(c) The microphone should not be carried by the user (e.g. on his body), but must be attached to the computer. In other words, the user should be restricted as little as possible.

Word chain recognition would enable the user to input commands verbally. This appears to be suitable for the expert user who can remember complex commands and who would be spared the trouble of typing in commands or their abbreviations (making typing errors at the same time).

Speaker-independent, continuous speech recognition opens up whole new applications, especially the direct translation of speech into text (the 'automatic typewriter' or 'speechwriter'). Such systems are not likely to emerge within the next ten years.

Table 7.2 — Techniques of speech processing

Technique	Application	Today	The future
		Speech	
Speech storage	—Voice mailing —Dictation —Spoken notes in documents —Non-simultaneous communication by speech	On the market Methods —delta modulation —LPC	Better compression techniques, giving more storage and better speech quality
Speech recognition —Word by word, speaker dependent	—HCI control via input commands —Telephone subscriber selection —AS control, e.g. electronic mailbox via telephone.	—Up to 500 word systems on market —Maximum speech length 2.5 s —Accuracy of recognition >98%	
—Word by word, speaker independent		10 numbers, 30–40 words	
—Word chains, speaker dependent	—Series of commands —Parameter inputs	40 connected words	500 word vocabulary, 200 word chains, each up to 5 words
—Word chains, speaker independent			50 word vocabulary
—Continuous, speaker dependent	—Automatic typewriter	—Up to 50 word systems on market —Accuracy of recognition >99%	
—Continuous, speaker independent		—Under development: <1300 word vocabulary [17]	Knowledge-based systems
Speech output	—Announcement and information systems		
Semi-synthetic —Uses text spoken by a human being (50× more efficient storage) —Excellent quality —System must know the vocabulary beforehand		On the market	
Fully synthetic	—Reading aloud any text over telephone	Available for English texts	Available for German

HCI = human–computer interface; AS = application system.

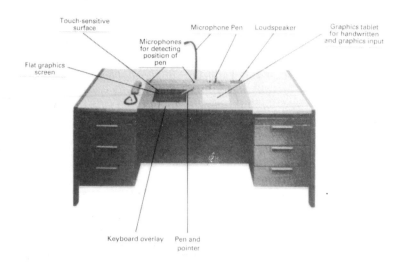

Fig. 7.14 — Experimental model of a manager's workstation.

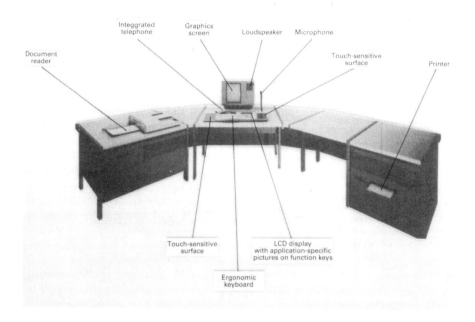

Fig. 7.15 — Experimental model of a secretary's workstation.

7.11   PICTURE PROCESSING

Static and moving pictures offer a new dimension of visual communication between human beings and computers. Video input would be via a special camera, with output to a colour graphics screen (in windows of any size, if required).

As well as for interpersonal communication, output of static and moving pictures would have important applications in tutorial systems for new users.

7.12   OUTPUT MEDIA

Output media will make increasing use of colour for the effective presentation of information. Large, flat, high resolution screens will also become readily available, although just how far the double A4 screen size will be exceeded is open to question. Larger screen displays would have to be mounted on the desk-top surface (like the touch-sensitive surfaces described above). An A4-size screen, however, seems to be the ergonomic minimum.

Another important output medium of the future is speech or, more generally, sound. We can distinguish between two kinds of speech output:

(a) output of digitally sorted speech
(b) output of fully synthetic speech (Fig. 7.16)

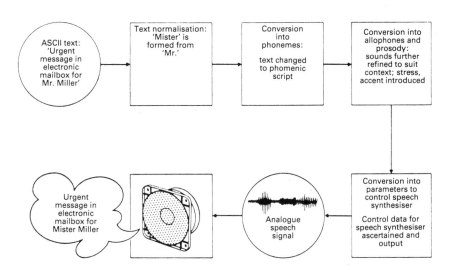

Fig. 7.16 — The principle of fully synthetic speech output.

In fully synthetic speech the computer constructs and synthesises the spoken output on the basis of an existing English text. The process involves several stages, but no genuine human voice is required, either as a model or as an object of reference.

Both types of speech output are very important for designing human –computer interfaces. Combined with sequences of pictures, output of digitally stored language and sound would be especially useful for tutorial systems.

Fully synthesised speech output can be used to give help messages and information and has the very practical advantage of drastically reducing the extent to which the user is tied to particular items of equipment and software. For example, the office manager may be waiting for an urgent communication in his electronic mail but finds himself tied up at his desk with meetings: it would be a great help to him if the computer could draw his attention to urgent electronic mail as soon as it arrives by outputting a spoken message.

7.13   SUMMARY

The input–output devices of today and tomorrow are opening up new possibilities for the design of interfaces which could make computers much easier to use. Above all, new technology is significantly extending the range of channels of communication, from seeing, typing, and pointing, to listening, speaking and writing by hand.

REFERENCES

[1] Anonymous (1983) *Computer Persönlich* (July 27) 13.
[2] Anonymous (1983) *Computer Persönlich* (September 21) 44–51.
[3] Anonymous (1983) *Computer Persönlich* (July 13) 114–150.
[4] Anonymous (1984) *Computer Persönlich* (January 25) 28–32.
[5] Anonymous (1984) *Computer* (February 8) 134–137.
[6] Anonymous (1984) *Computer* (January 11).
[7] Ohmann, F. (ed.) (1983) *Kommunikations-Endgeräte*, Springer, Berlin.
[8] Tafel, H. J. and Kohl, A. (1982) *Ein- und Ausgabegeräte der Datentechnik,* Carl Hanser.
[9] Trimuph Adler (1984) 7 Szenen aus dem Büro von morgen. *Videofilm,* Triumph Adler AG., Basisentwicklung.
[10] Anonymous (1984) *Computer Persönlich* (April 18).
[11] Anonymous (1982) *Markt Technik* (10) (March 12).
[12] Taylor, M. (198?) *Datamation.*
[13] Card, S. K., English, W. K. and Burr, B. (1977) Evaluation of mouse, rate-controlled isometric joystick, step keys and text keys for text selection on a crt. *Report SSL-77-1,* Xerox Palo Alto Research Center.
[14] Anonymous (1984) *Computerwoche* (December 14) 49.
[15] Anonymous (1985) *Datentechnik* (9) (April 30).
[16] Fähnrich, K. P. and Ziegler, J. (1983) *Office Management* (12) 1068–1075.
[17] Niemann, H. (1982) *Informatik-Fachberichte* 330–348.

8

Experience in designing user interfaces

W. Schweikhardt

8.1 SUMMARY

After differentiating between 'programmed instruction' and 'computer-assisted learning', we will discuss in this chapter the educational potential of the computer. After this we shall describe how we can use properly equipped computer-assisted systems to teach blind people new skills and to integrate them into working life.

8.2 INTRODUCTION

As members of the Applied Information Technology for the Blind research group at the Institute for Informatics at the University of Stuttgart, we have been developing computer-assisted aids to help blind people integrate into schools, universities and society in general. This work has been under way since 1978, although computers, of course, are only one of several vital contributions in the field.

An essential part of our work is concerned with the design of special user interfaces. Visual displays must be converted to audible or tactile forms via suitable output devices.

In the course of our research we have developed, among other things, a text processing system with an interface for both sighted and blind people. We have also designed and implemented a series of educational programs. These allow blind people to deepen the knowledge and skills which they have learned in class. We shall also see how blind people have been able to learn braille virtually without other external assistance. In 1980 a post for a blind programmer was established. The programmer works mainly on APL and is provided with an additional device developed from our research work in conjunction with a West German firm (Elektronische Hilfsmittel GmbH (formerly Schönherr), Brunnenstrasse 10, D-7240 Horb a. N.-Nordstetten). Special software for the programming interface was also necessary. The original workstation was equipped with an IBM 5100 microcomputer as the central processor.

In the meantime, blind people can now use the Teletext service of the West German Federal Post Office. This means that they have access to a large amount of information which, previously, they could only have if a sighted person was available to read it aloud to them. This has opened up a whole range of personal activities which sighted people take for granted. For example, they can exchange letters and messages with people who have no knowledge of braille and can enjoy direct and private access to a bank account.

In this chapter we explain how and with what devices a dialogue between a blind user and a computer can be carried out. We also discuss the essential design features for such an interface.

8.3 COMPUTER-ASSISTED LEARNING

The 1960s saw computer-assisted instruction (CAI) develop out of 'programmed instruction'. Nowadays we speak more generally of computer-assisted learning because the range of educational applications has become much broader. Apart from the pure transmission of information, the computer is used as a tool for developing practical and theoretical skills and for the simulation of events and situations.

In programmed instruction (as it appeared in books or on paper), a distinction was drawn between linear programs (B. F. Skinner) (Fig. 8.1) and branching programs (N. A. Crowder) (Fig. 8.2).

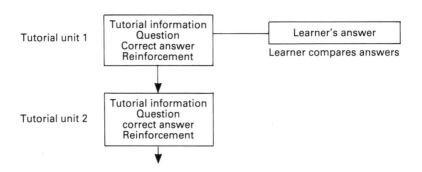

Fig. 8.1 — Linear program according to Skinner.

The program's responses were supposed to reinforce every correct answer given by the learner. In linear programs, the correct answers were stored by the computer. The program compared these with the learner's responses and would repeat a particular unit until the learner gave the expected (i.e. correct) input.

Very few educational objectives can be attained solely by the use of linear programs. For this reason Crowder developed the technique of

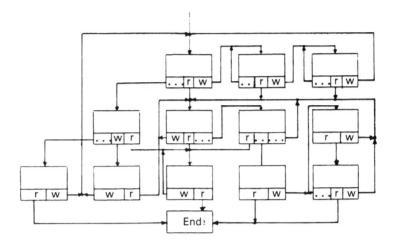

Fig. 8.2 — Example of a branching program according to Crowder: r, right response;
w, wrong response; . . ., other response.

branching programs. The essential difference is that, after completing a
unit, the learner can do more than either continue to the next unit in the
sequence or repeat the old one: he can branch to a special reinforcement unit
and take an individual path through the program which can be monitored by
the computer and recorded for the teacher.

Working from a book, the learner can page through and jump to
different parts of the 'program'. This can be provided on a computer by a
'command language' which the learner uses to tell the program the point
from which he would like to continue (e.g. tutorial unit or lesson).

The following CAI applications are worth noting.

(a) The PLATO project of the University of Illinois (USA). This has over
    2000 networked workstations and hundreds of educational programs
    with a wide variety of content. The users can also communicate with one
    another.
(b) Various applications in Japan. Very young children are using computers
    in schools, although the educational concepts are rather modest, despite
    the tremendous investment in hardware.
(c) In-house training systems for industry. These are in widespread use,
    leaders in the field being data processing firms and insurance
    companies.

In the Federal Republic of Germany, numerous CAI projects were
initiated in the early 1970s in colleges and other educational institutions.
Their success was limited because current mainframe computers were not
powerful enough and because the workstations (e.g. teletype terminals)
were inadequate for CAI.

Some applications, however, have been successful because they have restricted themselves to specific aspects of computer-assisted training. An example is the CAI system of the Foundation for Rehabilitation in Heidelberg. For several years this was the second largest CAI system in the world, with a series of notable innovations to its credit. Using an authoring system implemented in APL, the Foundation produced a large number of educational programs for learning and practising new skills and for simulations. The range of students was very diverse — handicapped people and rehabilitees — and the material was used to support various kinds of training course.

8.4 STRATEGIES IN COMPUTER-ASSISTED LEARNING

Modern mainframes and personal computers have a wide spectrum of facilities and devices for the end-user. These range from various programming languages to colour graphics screens, light pens, graphics tablets, etc. All this offers considerable potential for educationally sound computer-assisted learning.

8.4.1 Tutorial programs

The quality of a tutorial program depends on how carefully it has been designed and implemented. Good tutorial programs have the following features.

(a) The program generates questions automatically and will therefore ask different questions each time it is run. Which questions are generated can be made to depend on the learner's progress.
(b) During the course of his interaction with the computer, the learner progresses to new and more demanding material.
(c) The program can generate exercises automatically and in any desired quantity, allowing the learner to practise for as long as he wants.
(d) The learner can call up examples whenever he wishes.
(e) The program gives instructions and advice.

Output to the user is usually presented on a screen. With some equipment it is also possible to overlay this with video pictures or film, as in the West German Teletext system. Tutorial programs incorporating film material are already is use. Similarly, tape recorders can be computer linked to provide sound recordings.

When questions are presented to the learner, they should not be accompanied by a set of ready-made answers: the learner should have to formulate his response by himself. Although such responses are more difficult to analyse, the learner is forced to come to grips with the material and to assimilate it properly.

The usual input medium for responses is the computer keyboard. Given the advances being made in speech input devices, however, future systems will also be able to handle spoken responses.

Pointer, joysticks and touch-sensitive screens should be used with care.

They are justified where they simulate hand-held tools such as a rubber or scissors, or where they move something aside or stick it on (as in cutting and pasting operations in a text): drawing is another permissible application. They should not be used for choosing from menued lists of answers, or as any kind of substitute for verbal communication in tutorial interaction.

Example of a 'framework program' for computerised tutorials
A number of so-called 'authoring systems' are available to facilitate the preparation of tutorial programs. The instructor preparing the material (the author) needs no knowledge of programming. He inputs to the system the text material to be displayed (information and questions, etc.) and tells it the correct and incorrect answers which it can anticipate from the learner. The system is also told how to react to individual responses (i.e. whether to repeat the question or to continue with the tutorial from a certain point, etc.). Many systems make use of so-called MACROS, which are small subroutines to perform tasks such as input analysis, etc. (analysis routines are often written to ascertain whether a letter has been left out or the order of words is correct).

In our research program we have designed and implemented a so-called **framework program** (RAPRO) for writing tutorial programs which can be used with both blind and sighted learners. We have not called RAPRO an authoring system because the author must have some knowledge of the APL programming language in which RAPRO is implemented.

For each lesson, i, $1 < i < N$, an author setting up material with RAPRO is given four functions to complete. These specify two sets of items. The first is the following output to the learner:

— tutorial texts (function ΔiTEXT)
— questions (function ΔiQUESTIONS)
— exercises (function ΔiEXERCISE)

In the second set are the following items which will be available in the program:

— examples (function ΔiEXP)
— answer help (ΔiQUESTIONS and ΔiEXERCISES)
— answers or results (ΔiQUESTIONS AND ΔiEXERCISE)

If some exercises are to be generated by standard random methods while the program is running, the author must provide the variables and algorithms for these himself. In the ΔiQUESTIONS and ΔiEXERCISE functions, the author specifies the name of each analysis function. These can be taken from a library or he can write them himself. Fig. 8.3 shows the various components of RAPRO and how they interrelate.

The **central control** sets up the tutorial program: it asks the learner what he wants to do (via the dialogue processor) and calls the **manager function** which loads the lesson requested. In case of difficulties (e.g. insertion of the

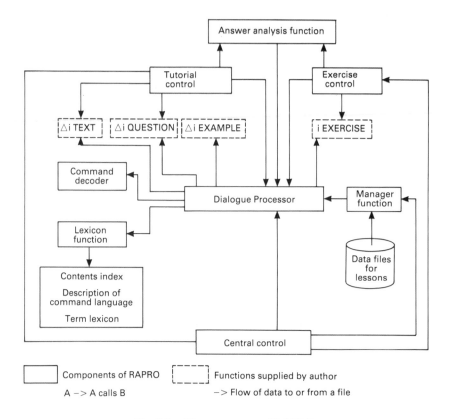

Fig. 8.3 — The components of RAPRO.

wrong diskette or no diskette at all), the control function goes back to the user with further questions. Once the lesson is loaded, control is handed over to the tutorial or exercise functions, whichever has been selected. The central control takes over again when the lesson is finished (or when the learner wants either another lesson or to end the session).

The manager function loads the lessons required from the secondary medium and keeps track of them.

The **dialogue processor** prepares output for whichever device has been selected. If, as is often the case in our own applications, the user is blind, then the output must be converted into a suitable form for him. This means that texts may have to be transformed into braille and sent to a special output device via a serial interface. This operation is discussed in more detail in section 8.4. The dialogue processor also receives input from the tutorial and exercise control functions and from the response analysis functions: the input arrives from the keyboard and is then made available to the calling function. If the input begins with the $ command sign, it is passed to the **command decoder** and the function which has been called is notified accordingly. The dialogue processor calls the function which corresponds to the result of the command analysis.

The author can enter in the **term lexicon** all the terms and their definitions which (a) are used in the tutorial program or (b) are new and have to be learned by the user. These terms are subsequently called by the **lexicon function**. If required, the lexicon function will provide the learner with a contents index of the lessons or a description of the user commands.

From the author functions ΔiTEXT and ΔiQUESTIONS, the **tutorial control** puts together an authoring sequence as illustrated in Fig. 8.4. From

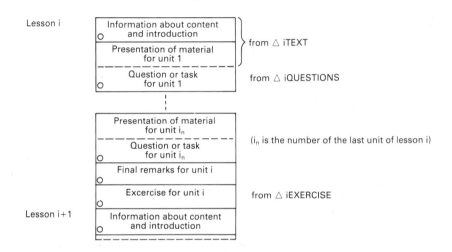

Fig. 8.4 — An authoring sequence (○ refers to points at which the user may input a command).

this, the user, by inputting the appropriate commands, can request examples from the ΔiEXP functions as well as clues or even the answer itself (from the ΔiQUESTIONS and ΔiEXERCISE functions). Moreover, he can follow a path through the tutorial which is more to his liking than that prescribed by the author.

Exercise control selects and presents to the learner one of the exercise types prepared by the author using ΔiEXERCISE. Within the set of exercises for a lesson, the author can prescribe different types of exercise which can be selected according to a fixed probability rate which he sets beforehand. It is up to the user when he wants to leave an exercise and to return to the central control function.

Command language

Commands always begin with the $ sign. The first letter of the command itself must be correct: thereafter the user is allowed to type in one letter wrongly, one too many or too few, and two characters may be transposed. Commands may also be abbreviated, the minimum form being the initial letter.

Below are listed the set of legal commands. The reader should see from these the extent to which the learner is able to direct his own path through the tutorial program and the sort of help facilities which are available to him. Of particular importance is the $QUESTION command, by which he can call up the text of the current exercise for reference, and the $TERM command, which gives him access to the lexicon of terms used in the tutorial.

Command	Effect of command
$ANSWER	Output correct answer to the last question.
$EXP	Output example illustrating the material of the current unit. Produces different examples each time it is called. This command has no effect during an exercise.
$END	End lesson or exercise.
$QUESTION	Output again the text of the last question.
$CONTENT	Output contents index.
$JUMP	Leave the current lesson or exercise. The user can return to this point later with $BACK.
$CLUE	Output a clue to the last question. More assistance is given if the command is used repeatedly.
$RLU	Repeat last unit.
$BACK	Return to the last point left by $JUMP.
$?	Output a summary of the command language.
$TERM	Output a definition of a given term.

The first version of RAPRO was designed and implemented as part of a diploma project for the Institute of Informatics at the University of Stuttgart [1]. From this version, four lessons were produced for a demonstration tutorial program called BRURE, an introduction to using fractions. We have also used RAPRO to construct a tutorial on how to perform mathematical calculations with whole numbers.

Thanks to a new graphics output device for the blind, we have been able to use RAPRO to provide blind people with a tactile understanding of basic two-dimensional concepts in geometry (point, distance, straight line, polygon, circle and ellipse) and of bodies on the horizontal plane.

There is an urgent need to provide blind people with the appropriate knowledge and expertise in this particular area if they are to take advantage of careers in data processing.

8.4.2 Simulations

The ability of modern computers to display colour and movement on the screen opens the door to a variety of so-called simulation procedures. The object of a simulation is to give a dynamic illustration of a process or an event. The processes may be an experiment in physics or chemistry, or be taken from biology (e.g. the laws of heredity). Business management and economics can also provide suitable models for simulation.

A computerised simulation should be fast enough to prevent the learner from becoming bored by having to wait too long for the next event to happen. Indeed, the simplest example of a simulation is a film. The learner should also be able to alter the speed of a simulation so that he can properly observe what is happening and understand the effects of his own input parameters to the underlying model.

In the future, simulations will be used in training the handicapped, especially those with impaired vision and hearing. Graphics and moving pictures, for example, can already be conveyed to blind people by means of an electronic peg-board on which the pegs are moved up and down by a computer [2]. Using such techniques of tactile perception, it is possible to simulate certain experiments in science teaching which would normally rely on hearing or smell. The hard of hearing and especially the totally deaf could enjoy new access to ideas and concepts normally expressed by spoken language.

8.5   USER INTERFACES FOR THE HANDICAPPED

A suitably adapted computer can often help human beings with physical handicaps and communication problems to compensate for their disability.

Oversize keyboards are available with motor handicaps. Input can also be initiated with the aid of rods or sticks which can be attached to the mouth or the head.

For the visually handicapped, magnifying devices are available which can project the contents of a screen onto a television set. The user can magnify part of the screen up to almost any size and often has a choice of colour combination (manufactured by two West German firms: Baum Elektronik GmbH, Schloss Langenzell, 6901 Wiesenbach, and Reinecker Videotechnick GmbH, Darmstädter Strasse 3, D-6101 Bickenbach).

For blind people there are also braille pointers, printers and, since 1985, even devices for outputting graphics in tactile form.

Data processing has opened up a new range of professions for the disabled. Data-handling peripheral devices and workstations can be adapted to give handicapped people greater opportunities for learning new skills and for participating more effectively in the world of everyday work.

8.5.1   Communication between a blind person and a computer

Communication between a human being and a computer requires suitable input–output devices. Experienced typists can work 'blind'. Similarly, a genuinely blind person can learn how to use the computer keyboard. Joysticks can also be used by the blind for cursor control and choosing items from a screen menu [3]. In Stuttgart we are developing touch-sensitive input devices for the blind.

The improvement in the quality of speech output devices and their low cost compared with equipment for outputting braille would appear at first glance to make them ideal for simulating screen contents for the blind. For many blind users, however, speech output will continue to be the only possible way to understand computer output. This is especially true for those who find it too difficult to learn braille or who are losing their sense of touch.

It is essential, therefore, that output which normally appears on a screen is converted into a form which a blind person can understand. With current technology, there are two ways of representing screen contents, i.e. in tactile and audible form.

8.5.1.1 Audible reproduction of screen contents

Screen contents are made up of graphics and alphanumeric characters. If a speech output device is to 'read aloud' strings of alphanumeric characters, then the character sequences have to be converted to words and numbers. Some way must also be found to convert punctuation and special characters into sounds.

The following examples illustrate some of the difficulties involved.

Representation on screen	*Speech output*
125	one *hundred* and twentyfive
12.125	*twelve* point one two five
the 1st day	the first *day*
on the 1st day	on the first *day*
The values differ by 6.12	. . . by six point one *two*
Next session on 6.12	. . . on the sixth of the *twelfth*
At 6.12	at six *twelve*
incl.	inclusive

Tables will have to be recognised and read out as ordered items, e.g.

Monthly profile	Branch	Number
Sales of article X	North	1 234
in each branch of	West	526
the city	South	2 145
	East	1 134

This is an example of a screen whose contents cannot be read aloud line by line.

Graphics cannot be represented in spoken form unless the pictures are described verbally. There is, however, no known facility for doing this, i.e. no suitable data bases with models of graphic patterns and their possible meanings, or rules able to derive such meanings and generate speech output. On the basis of current models we can certainly conceive of speech output being suitable for specific applications, such as to represent bar and pie charts. However, the author of this chapter considers the reading aloud of screen displays in general (e.g. teletext graphics) to be impossible.

Apart from the problems already mentioned, acoustic representation has further disadvantages. The listener would not have full control over the rate of output, nor would he be able to pick out certain parts of it in the way that a sighted user looks at a display on a screen. This is bound to place heavy demands on his powers of concentration and attentiveness. Moreover, a blind person will want to call up information which is specifically meant for him: this would have to be done via headphones. Many people, however, are not happy using headphones and blind people need their hearing to detect noises in their general surroundings.

For a wide variety of reasons, many of the 75 000 blind persons in West Germany are unable to use braille. For this reason we have devoted some effort to converting screen displays of text to audible form, despite the disadvantages and difficulties already mentioned. In software developed in Stuttgart, graphics are reduced to tactile representations and everything else is reproduced as speech [4].

As a rule, blind people prefer to use braille to read information which would normally be presented to a sighted person in written form. Speech output which would be acceptable to a sighted person would be equally well received by someone who is blind.

8.5.1.2 Tactile reproduction of screen contents
In our opinion there is no satisfactory alternative to representing screen contents in tactile form. The system of braille which is now used throughout the world is based on the six-dot writing scheme invented by Louise Braille (1809–1852). A subset of these dots is used to represent a particular character, e.g.

These dots are printed onto braille paper (a thin card). In modern electronic output devices, pins made of metal or synthetic material can be moved in such a way that 'raised' dots can be detected by human touch, while the remaining pins remain depressed.

All the letters of the Roman alphabet and all punctuation signs have counterparts in braille, for which there is an international standard. There are also special signs for national languages, such as the German characters, ß, ä, ö, ü.

There is a distinction between full braille and abbreviated braille. Even in full braille, which is learned by primary schoolchildren and by people who become blind later in life, typical sound groups specific to the language are abbreviated to a single braille character (e.g. ph, ion, ed). For this reason alone a blind person has difficulty reading sequences of braille letters which have been converted character by character from ordinary writing. Most blind people use the abbreviated version, which is taught to older schoolchildren. Texts in abbreviated braille are on average 30% shorter than full braille. Conventions for this version include abbreviations for sound groups, initial and final syllables, word stems and full words. Words have the highest priority, sound groups the lowest. Within these groups there are supplementary rules and other rules indicating priorities. The pronunciation of words is also taken into account, e.g. *ough* as in *cough* and *though*.

Braille for dialogue between the computer and the blind user
When coding braille texts for blind users we must take account of the following.

(a) In braille 64 different characters are represented by 64 different combinations of dots. These are not enough to represent all the special characters, such as mathematical symbols. Even more importantly, they are not enough for all the characters used in programming languages and which can be input from a microcomputer keyboard.
(b) National languages have their own rules of abbreviation.

Many blind computer users expect texts to appear in braille form, and for mathematical expressions it is customary to use mathematical braille. If the interaction requires a high level of user activity, blind people will also accept short (e.g. single line) output in full braille or even in the form of a character-by-character translation. Most users, however, will reject longer texts output in this way, particularly for help information or for examples in tutorial programs.

A blind person can only control his own input if each typed character can be represented in braille. Since each character input via the keyboard must correspond to a single braille sign, the 6-dot script had to be expanded into an 8-dot system. Here, the standard braille alphabet is used to represent lower case letters. Upper case letters, which are not distinguished in standard braille, are characterised by adding dot 7 (see Fig. 8.5).

```
1  ○  ○  4        ○  ×        ○  ×
2  ○  ○  5        ×  ×        ×  ×
3  ○  ○  6        ×  ○        ×  ○
7  ○  ○  8        ○  ○        ×  ○
                     t           T
```

Fig. 8.5 — Numbered dots for the braille characters t and T. × represents a raised dot detectable by touch.

This convention has become established for blind people involved in data processing applications. There is also a coding system for the characters of the APL programming language [5] which is compatible with Stuttgart mathematical braille [6] and with our own proposal for a tactile version of the CEPT standard characters used in European videotex systems [7].

On the screen, an alphanumeric character (including the distance to adjacent characters) takes up the same space as a non-alphanumeric graphic character. To position both text and graphics correctly on the same screen, braille text and braille graphic characters must also be of equal size. However, non-alphanumeric characters should not be separated by lines and spaces, as alphanumeric braille characters are.

We have devised a system of coding which assigns to each character a subset of raised dots in a 5×3 matrix. An alphanumeric character is represented by the 8 dots of the top 4 lines and first 2 rows, while all 15 dots are available for non-alphanumeric graphic characters.

Fig. 8.6 shows the different types of non-alphanumeric characters as they

—Block graphics characters

—Diagonal graphics characters

—Line graphics characters

—User-defined graphics characters
 (e.g. with 10×6 dots)

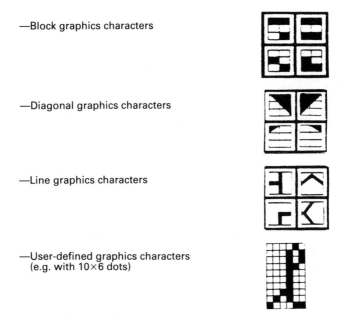

Fig. 8.6 — Types of non-alphanumeric graphic characters.

appear on screen. Fig. 8.7 gives some examples of our coding of CEPT standard characters. For a complete list of codes see [7].

8.5.2 The Stuttgart pilot configuration for the computer-assisted tactile reproduction of screen contents

The central processor for our pilot configuration (see Fig. 8.8) is an IBM PC XT microcomputer with a disk drive and 10 MB hard disk. For input we use a commonly available commercial keyboard. A braille keyboard can be added on.

The dialogue between the blind user and the program takes place via the

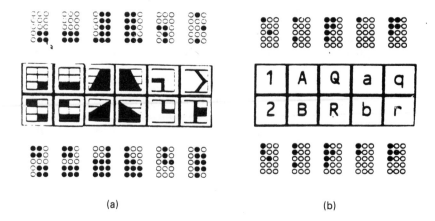

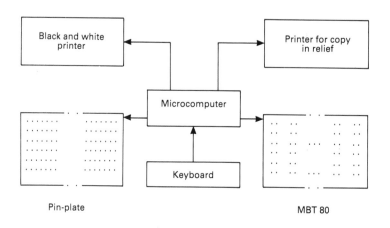

(a)   (b)

Fig. 8.7 — Examples of codes for (a) block, diagonal and line non-alphanumeric graphic characters and (b) alphanumeric characters conforming to the European videotex standard.

Fig. 8.8 — The Stuttgart pilot configuration of the computer-assisted tactile reproduction of screen contents.

keyboard and an MBT 80 braille output device (produced by the Deutsche Blindenstudienanstalt Elektronik und Hilfsmittel GmbH, Brunnenstrasse 10, D-7240 Horb a.N.-Nordstetten, West Germany). This device can output two 40-character lines at a time and has a built-in memory for a further 70 lines which can be displayed via a special keyboard in the device itself.

Graphics are reproduced on an electronically controlled pin-plate. This contains 59 lines of pins of 119 pins each which can be raised and lowered individually by the computer (produced by METEC GmbH, Senefelder-stasse 77a, D-7000 Stuttgart 1, West Germany). Each configuration on the pin-plate can be output in braille by a BETA X3 relief printer (produced by Thiel GmbH & Co. KG, Industrie-Electronic, Pauerweg, Postfach 88, D-6104 Seeheim-Jugenheim, West Germany).

All output devices for blind users are linked to the computer by serial interfaces. The transmission rate is in each case 9600 baud.

8.6 CONCLUDING REMARKS

Computer-assisted learning is effective for self-tuition and in the acquisition of skills. It comes into its own where it is not practicable to teach a group (e.g. in distance learning or where the group would be too small) or where a lot of individual tuition is required (e.g. students have to practise what they have learned in class, as in reading and writing braille).

Although the technical resources for effective computer-assisted learning are available, it often fails because the laborious task of properly designing and implementing the software is neglected. Further development of authoring systems is urgently needed if we are to have more efficient and higher quality tutorial systems.

Designing user interfaces for the handicapped is a highly worthwhile task in which information scientists and educationalists from various specialist disciplines must work together. Only through their mutual cooperation will we end up with effective hardware and software which can be used both in training centres and the workplace.

REFERENCES

[1] Kohns, M. (1980) *Diploma Thesis*, Institute for Informatics, University of Stuttgart.

[2] Bleischwitz, W. (1985) *Diploma Thesis*, Institute for Informatics, University of Stuttgart.

[3] Dürre, K. P. and Schmidt-Lademann, F.-P. (1983) Interactive computer interfaces for the blind. *Proceedings of the IEEE Computer Society Workshop on Computers in the Education and Employment of the Handicapped, Minneapolis, Minnesota*, pp. 89–96.

[4] Mayer, E. (1986) *Diploma Thesis*, Institute for Informatics, University of Stuttgart.

[5] Schweikhardt, W. (1983) 8-dot braille for representing information from computers. *Proceedings of the IEEE Computer Society Workshop on Computers in the Education and Employment of the Handicapped, Minneapolis, Minnesota*, pp. 85–88.

[6] Schweikhardt, W. (1982) A programming environment for blind APL programmers. *APL 82 Conference Proceedings, APL Quote Quad* **13** (1) 325–331.

[7] Schweikhardt, W. (1985) *Report*, Institute for Informatics, University of Stuttgart.

The contributors

Main authors

Professor H.-J. Bullinger
Frauenhofer Institute for Organisation and Methods, Holzgartenstrasse 17,
7000 Stuttgart 1, West Germany

Professor Rul Gunzenhäuser
Institute of Informatics at the University of Stuttgart, Azenbergstrasse 12,
7000 Stuttgart 1, West Germany

Other authors

Dr. Helmut Balzert
Triumph-Adler AG, Fürther Strasse 212, 8500 Nuremberg 80, West
Germany.

Dr. Heike von Benda
Ministry of Economics and Technology, Theodor-Heuss-Strasse 4, 7000
Stuttgart 1, West Germany

Klaus-Peter Fähnrich
Frauenhofer Institute for Organisation and Methods, Holzgartenstrasse 17,
7000 Stuttgart 1, West Germany

Professor Gerhard Fischer
Department of Computer Science, University of Colorado,. Boulder,
ECOT 7-7 Engineering Center, Campus Box 430, Boulder, CO 80309, USA

Dr. Waltraud Schweikhardt
Institute for Informatics at the University of Stuttgart, Azenbergstrasse 12,
7000 Stuttgart 1, West Germany

Jürgen Ziegler
Frauenhofer Institute for Organisation and Methods, Holzgartenstrasse 17,
7000 Stuttgart 1, West Germany

Index

APL, 121, 124, 132
Application, specification of representation, 18
Attentiveness, 92, 96
Authoring sequence, 127

Blind users, 129
Braille, 131
Braille output device, 130, 134

Character-oriented dialogue, 66
Command language, 127
Command language grammar (CLG), 15
Computers, hostility to, 91
Computer-assisted learning, 122f, 124f
Convivial systems, 91

Data field oriented dialogue, 66
Description, techniques of, 33
Design, methods of, 32f
Dialogue,
    generator, 50, 53
    knowledge-based, 77f
    natural language, 43f
    simulator, 49f
    switching between forms of, 44
    system, 20
    versions, 67f
Digitiser, 108f
Dipmeter, 96
Direct manipulation, *see* icons and pointers
DYNAFORM, 99

Elicitation of information, 33
ELIZA, 78
Error and help messages, 68
Evaluation, methods of, 33
Expert systems, 95ff

Filter 96, 99
FINANCE, 98f
Form generator, 53
Form input (on screen) 42, 47, 52ff

GEM, 20f
Gestalt theory, 54f
GOMS model, 15
Graphics tablet, 107f

Handicapped users, 129
Handwritten input, 112ff
Hardware, 91f
Help key, 46
Help systems, 32, 35, 79ff
Human-computer interaction, 89ff

Icons and pointers, 18, 23f, 32, 35, 42, 43, 44f, 47, 114
Illich, Ivan, 91
Information, visual, 93
Input command, 58
Input/output
    devices, 102ff
    system, 19
Instructions to user, simple/multiple, 42f
Intelligent workstation, 65
Interrupt key, 46
ISO-OSI model, 15

Joystick, 104f

Knowledge,
    acquisition of, 96
    base, 95ff
    using, 96f

Laws of gestalt theory, 54f

ELLIS HORWOOD BOOKS IN COMPUTING SCIENCE
General Editors: Professor JOHN CAMPBELL, University College London, and BRIAN L. MEEK, Director of Information Technology, Goldsmiths' College, London, and King's College London (KQC), University of London
Series in Computers and Their Applications
Series Editor: BRIAN L. MEEK, Director of Information Technology, Goldsmiths' College, London, and King's College London (KQC), University of London

Computer Communications and Networking